PIE FOR BREAKFAST

Reminiscences of a Farmhand

by

HARRY REFFOLD

HUTTON PRESS

1984

Printed by Clifford Ward & Co.
(Bridlington) Ltd.

Hutton Press Ltd.,
130 Canada Drive, Cherry Burton, Beverley,
North Humberside, HU17 7SB.

Reprinted 1986, 1988, 1994

ISBN 0 907033 17 2

FOREWORD

For a number of years I have had the pleasure of being the guest speaker at various organisations in the East Riding, reminiscing about my early days as a farmhand. As the years passed, I realised that the number of people who knew the days before 1914 were getting fewer and people were beginning to think of that era as being romantic. I have written this book to show that it was far from romantic, but we had fun — and love has always been the same.

I dedicate this book to my wife, Marie, who encouraged me to write it and then typed it for me. She was a "townie," but has enjoyed every moment of the time we have lived in the country.

ABOUT THE AUTHOR

Harry Reffold was born and brought up in Driffield and, like most of the lads in the town, on reaching the age of 14 went to work on one of the local farms. He worked on farms until after the First World War when he left the country to work in the city. His ambition was always to return to the country and this he did on his retirement.

The author's letters to school children on life in the country are the subject of his first book, "Countryman's Diary — Letters from a Hull School."

LIST OF ILLUSTRATIONS

CHAPTER ONE

It seems a long time ago — in fact it is a long time ago, but I remember it well, that Autumn of 1914. Thousands of young farmworkers had left the farms on which they were working and had joined the army for, as most of us fondly thought, a few months. Besides, it would be a nice change to spend a few weeks learning to march, use a rifle and then, if it wasn't all over, a trip to France and then into Germany just to finish off the Kaiser and then back home. When we look today at the village war memorials we can see the reality of the situation.

In those days the only way for a hired man to leave his employer legally between one Martinmas and the next, the following year, and to be paid the full amount that he had earned was for him either to die or join the army — illness made no difference. He was a hired man, and as such his employer, the farmer, had to feed and keep him and provide a doctor. If it was a serious illness — say a broken leg or something that was going to be a long job — then the patient was usually pushed off home, or if that was not possible, it was into the Workhouse Hospital. Sickness was not encouraged, and sympathy was very scarce.

By the time Martinmas hirings in November 1914 were over and the recruiting campaign had got into full swing, very few farmers had been able to hire sufficient labour to be able to work the land, so it was no surprise when one day the headmaster at our school announced: "Any boy who has turned twelve years of age may leave school immediately, providing he can pass an examination to prove he can read and write, and providing that he will promise to go and work on a farm."

Well, I was thirteen and in Standard Six, and good at both subjects, so I just couldn't get home fast enough to tell them all about it and how I could leave the next day and go out and earn lots of money — but it didn't work out that way.

I was born in the small country town of Driffield in East Yorkshire. Father had been a farmhand but, at about the age of twenty, he had missed getting hired at the Martinmas hirings. This inevitably meant the Winter out of work except for the odd day's threshing on the local farms, or sometimes casual work for the local council or small firms.

No work meant no money, but we had in our town two small flour mills which were always wanting men. Some said it was because the conditions under which the men worked and the low wages they were paid ensured that someone was either ill or leaving each week. So Father got himself a job at one of the flour mills to see the Winter over, but when I arrived, one more mouth meant that more money was wanted, so he decided to go to Leeds to try his luck on the railway. This meant another five shillings a week more — not much these days, but then it was a lot of money, and besides, years later, I changed jobs and my future for just two shillings a week extra.

As my father had an older brother married and working in Leeds on the railway, he had a home with them until he found a house and could send for my mother and me to join him.

Mother had a fiery temper, but Dad was easy-going until roused, and then he became really vicious. I can still remember the rows and the squabbles that became more regular until the day when Dad was taken ill with rheumatic fever and was very ill for a long time.

Again, it was a question of no work, no money, so Mother had to go out to work in one of the many clothing "sweat" shops, as they were called, in Leeds, where the women were on piece work and had to put twelve hours a day in to get a living wage. By this time I had a sister too, which did not make things any easier. So I was pushed back to Grandmother to a country life which I thought was super, as I had regularly spent my school holidays with her. By this time I was seven.

Grandmother was nearly eighty when I went to her. She was a kindly, affectionate soul who doted on me and who had been a widow for a number of years. She had had a tough life, with a large number of children — five boys and five girls living. I don't know how many had died, because in those days the doctor had to be paid for any visits or medicine provided, and more often than not the baby died before the money was raised for medical attention. Many doctors in country areas did on occasions go easy on their bills, but eighty years ago consumption was rampant, and very few families in country or town were free from someone who suffered from the disease.

I quite well remember my own relief at reaching the age of twenty without catching consumption, for it was a widely held belief that if you passed that age you stood a good chance of missing it. Unfortunately it did not always work out that way. The youth of today should go on their knees and give thanks for the virtual elimination of the disease. Grandmother lost one son and one daughter through it, and many a woman had lost her husband and was left with babies and a doctor's bill to pay and only the workhouse to look forward to.

The "grubber," as it was usually called in those days, was a big house where the women toiled from daylight to dark, mostly washing clothes for the inmates and also for the workhouse hospital. The men had a fixed amount of wood to chop and bundle up for sale to the shops in the town. I can remember the two-wheeled handcart which two of the inmates used to pull around delivering to the customers. The children grew up under a very strict discipline, and were sent out to work at the first opportunity. Age did not matter so long as someone would take them and feed them and look after them, and in general the type of work did not matter either. Quite regularly the local sweeps got their apprentices from the workhouse, as did some of the local cowkeepers, where a 5 a.m. start was the norm and knocking-off time was when all was finished after tea and pay was an afterthought. The girls went without any to-do whatsoever straight into domestic service, the only difference being that those with a bit of character went to the better houses.

I sometimes walk down the avenue leading to the new school, a huge building in acres of grassland, with football pitches and all outdoor sports catered for and also a swimming pool. I look at the pupils wandering their way there, big, well-built boys and girls, bright-eyed and confident, the odd one or two arm in arm with looks only for one another, and for the rest, their only worry is their "O" levels. I reflect that seventy or less years ago most of the girls would have been bound for domestic service, the rest for the local rug factory, the laundry, or the few town shops, and the boys would have been hired farmhands or apprentices to the various local industries, and all those magical holidays abroad were not even a vision. In my youth, only the odd schoolmaster got as far as the Continent. I remember one of our own teachers, when I was a child, going to Germany. This was regarded as fantastic, and he got due hero-worship for a while when he returned to school.

My school was a Church of England school built in the traditional brick with three small classrooms and one large room which held Standards Three, Four, Six and Seven. The headmaster was a tall, thin Scotsman who had lost his accent but not his taste for his country's prime product, and after the lunchtime break at the Black Swan, he could and did wield the cane with the ferocity with which any of his ancesters might have wielded a sword. But old Pat was respected, and any lad who got into trouble with authority was immediately expelled and told to go to the other school, which was the local board council school.

We quite liked the rest of the staff, three men and two women, except for one whom no-one liked, not even the other teachers, and much less me after I had been given a thump on the ear with a clenched fist for some spelling error. The blow burst an eardrum and caused permanent deafness in that ear years later. There would be a commotion if it happened now, and that is why I look with envy at those well-built young people walking up the school avenue.

Uncle Dick was Grandmother's oldest child and a bachelor to his death at the age of eighty. He started work in the local oil and cattle-cake mill at the age of twelve, and never learnt to read or write, so either myself or Grandma used to read the paper to him. But his favourite pastime was poaching, and he had plenty of time for that because the oil mill used to close down or go on short time in Summer when the demand from the farmers for feeding cake for their cattle was low. As labour was cheap and plentiful the company just told the men: "Don't come in the morning, come next week." Once again, no work meant no money, so Dick and some of his cronies became the scourge of the gamekeepers and, of course, the police.

I still remember his gun. It used to break into two parts and hung from a special belt inside his shirt, one part down each trouser leg. I also remember his heavy fustin jacket with the poacher's pocket running right round the inside lining so that a bird or rabbit laid in it hardly showed.

For many years he courted a tall good-looking woman, and she turned him from a hard drinker and liver into a really smart chap. She also go him going to Church—a thing he had never done before. But it was a Catholic church, and Grandma and all the rest of the family were Protestants, so all the old prejudices and bigotry of the two families came out in full, and what could have been a happy union turned sour.

Then, to cap all, his oldest sister, Aunt Polly, who was working in a London mental asylum, married and ex-Irish guardsman who was a true Catholic too. That shattered the whole family, particuarly when she came home to have her baby and had him christened at our local Catholic church. She then left little James with her Aunt Jane, who was Grandma's sister, and went back to her living-in job at the hospital. She could not leave her baby with her mother, as by this time Grandma had been burdened with John, a little mistake that her third daughter had made!

About this time Grandfather worked for a local timber firm leading timber from the woods with the old style wood wagon. This was a four-wheeled vehicle, the forerunner of our modern artic, which had front wheels with a turntable on top and a ten-inch diameter pole fastened with a metal loop and pin to the front axle. The rear axle could be extended to any length of the pole and fastened by metal pins going through holes in the pole, thus checking any movement forward or back so that any length of tree could be loaded onto it. Then the horses were yoked, and anyone who has not seen a team of horses, all Shires, maybe six of them, with their heads down as they strained to pull the wagon loaded with a huge tree trunk across a field, has missed one of the most beautiful sights ever. The last of them moved out a few years ago, and the team and the drivers will never return.

There was no retirement in those days, and Lloyd George was only a young man with an idea, so most men just kept working — or, as the saying was, carried their nosebags — until they dropped, and Grandad was almost seventy when a tree trunk dropped onto his leg. Having seen many accidents on farms and what happens, I can visualise what would follow. There would most likely be a maximum of five men, including two wood fellers and one horseman. It was usual for two drivers, each with a team of three horses, to be loading and working together. To be able to do any rescue they would first have to lift the trunk, so they would have to dismantle the tree-lifting gear, which, if it had been lifting heavy timber, would have a heavy steel block and chain fastened to it and would require a spanner to undo the screw nuts. If it had been lifting light trunks, it would have double wood blocks and a long rope so that they could yoke a horse to the rope, thus making an easy job of lifting the timber onto the wagons.

By this time Grandad would be in a state of shock, which no-one would know about or bother about, no matter what the weather, even if it was snowing or raining. Eventually the trunk would be lifted, and then they would think about moving him. One of the men would go to the nearest farm to borrow a horse and rully and a few sacks to lay him on in order to take him to hospital, which in his case was his own town workhouse hospital, where the doctor duly took his leg off. He must have been a tough old chap because he lived a few years after that and died of pneumonia, leaving Grandma a widow and quite a large doctor's bill.

CHAPTER TWO

It was 1908 and Dada was just about better and ready for work and I was still with Grandmother. Mother had been sending her half a crown per week to keep me, and with Uncle Dick's ten shillings a week board (when he had it) Grandma was managing very nicely, so when the question of me going back to Leeds came up, it was decided that if I wanted to I could stay where I was. I had never wanted to go back at any time, even when I had holidays.

My cousin John had now started work as an apprentice. He was still with Grandma, but his mother had married and had had a further three boys and six girls. James, the odd one out, the Catholic, who by this time was in a good trade and was the only one who ever gave me any extra pocket money (my pocket money in those days was one halfpenny on Thursday, Market Day, and another one on Saturday. A penny was a lot of money in those days, and I willingly cleaned his bicycle and his button boots for him — most children would do an awful lots of jobs for a penny!) James's aunt completely spoilt him, and he grew up with a great liking for drink.

Aunt Jane, who was Grandma's sister, and Uncle Kerry used to keep the Bay Horse Inn. It was the first pub in the town coming from the north or west roads and had quite a good weekend trade when the farmhands came into town to do their shopping and to have the odd pint and talk a bit of farming with their pals.

The Bay Horse was one of the small country pubs you now only see in pictures, right on the pavement edge with three steps from the path into the passage. The first door on the left was the bar entrance; the door on the right was the smokeroom, and at the end was a little snug where special customers could and did drink all night and play cards. The snug had no windows to the outside so no-one could check. There had originally been three cottages at one end, and these had been turned into a small common lodging house where tramps or down-and-outs could stay the night and cook anything that would cook over the huge fireplace at one end of the long kitchen, which was the three downstairs rooms knocked into one. The upstairs had been opened up in the same way.

The place was looked after by a man who had only one arm and who also had the lower part of his leg missing. He was always known as "Soldier." He kept the place tidy and took each man's money — tuppence per night, one shilling per week, and an extra halfpenny for a clean pillowcase. It was poor, but it was home for a few of the — in those days — many people who had no home of their own and who were too old or poorly to work and would put up with anything rather than go into the workhouse. One could see them most days either begging or hunting round for old rags and metal, or better still, old bones, which fetched a good price at the rag and bone shop. There was at that time a great demand for bones, which were crushed and sold as fertiliser to the farmers.

At the rear of the pub were the usual buildings — stables for the horses that came in on Market Day drawing the carriers' wagons which would be parked in the Market Place. The wagons were usually light four-wheeled vehicles with a cover over them, and the carriers themselves were a hardy breed of countrymen who rose early on Market Days and collected goods such as butter and eggs from the farms and delivered them to the shops in the market town.

The wagons would also take a few of the village women on their shopping expeditions. We who are now used to having a bus route through most villages, even if it is sometimes infrequent, can hardly imagine anyone sitting under a tarpaulin on a wooden bench, starting off at 6 a.m., while the horses trundled their way probably six or more miles, calling at various farms on the way and doing the same on the way back, just so that they could buy something they could not get in the village shop.

Also at the rear of the pub was a barn — one of the old flail barns where the gleaners could bring their gleanings from the cornfields to be flailed. The old barn was what would now be a conservationist's dream. There was a flailing floor, raised about six inches above the barn floor, which was made of flat sandstone. It was about eight feet in diameter, with a stone walking path round it. Cut into the stone floor were the corn grooves where the flailed corn gathered.

Outside was a capstan-like post that one could yoke a horse to, set it going, and by cogs and rods and wheels etc. work the various machines inside. The first one was a grinding mill. It had two rollers and a feed box above it, and as the corn was flailed it was gathered up and put into the winnowing machine alongside the mill and driven by another shaft and belt which turned a system of flat boards round the inside. As the corn dropped down it met a gust of air from the rotation of the boards. The chaff was blown out and light corn blown onto a shelf and dropped behind the machine while the sound corn fell into a bag which hung on the front.

Towards the end of the eighteen hundreds Uncle Kerry had one of the new threshing machines put into the barn. It was driven by two horses to get the higher speed required to turn the threshing drum, and of course this also dispensed with two men from the flailing floor and did the work ten times quicker. He also had a Bamlett horse-drawn reaper. I can well remember Grandma telling me that a policeman had to come when he first used it because the local men were sure it would put them out of work for ever, and there was nearly a riot, but there the machines were in the barn when I was a boy.

There were also some of the flails hung on the walls, but a few years later progress, as it is called, caught up with the old pub and it was pulled down. The barn and its contents suffered the same fate. The machines were broken up, the scrap metal taken to the rag shop, and the woodwork from the whole site burned. All the old brickwork went into the footings of a big new Bay Horse Inn with a large car park and no stables. It is over fifty years ago since it happened, but the memory lingers on.

Aunt Jane and her husband, Kerry, had the Bay Horse for a number of years until about 1885. One Saturday evening during harvest time, with a full house of labourers and others, a party of Irish harvesters came in, and in the ensuing crush a fight started. Uncle, well-known as a tough handful, started to put some of the rowdies out. In the melee that followed one of the Irishmen bit his thumb, and as there was no knowledge of antiseptics in those days, the almost inevitable blood-poisoning set in — that red streak pushing up the arm that even myself as a young lad used to dread, and the result, a blood-poisoned system which left Uncle Kerry blind and deaf.

He was still alive, but a very old man when I went back to Grandma. He lived a few doors from her and I remember he used to walk up and down the garden path, sometimes gently singing a hymn to himself and we used to write little messages to him on the palm of his hand — a rather laborious method, but it was a means of communication.

Every week I had to go for father's eggs. He was now back at work on the railway on Leeds station, and Grandmother would give me a shilling to go to a distant relation. She always used to remind me to call him "uncle." He had a little pub and farm about half a mile from the town, and in his spare time he did a bit of horse-breaking. He had a board on the pub wall telling all and sundry that he took "Light horses or draught horses, gentled them, broke them in to all gears or saddles and guaranteed a good mouth." There was an old snubbing post on the green just opposite his front entrance where he did most of the breaking in, with a horse on a ten foot fixed line from the bridle to the ring on the top of the post so that a horse could be driven round and round with a pair of long reins, or strings as they were called, until it answered to spoken commands.

It was quite a long job breaking a horse in because it first had to have a 'mouth,' that is, it had to get used to having a bit, called a mouthing bit, a heavy one usually with a small piece of chain in the centre. The horse would be stood in the stable, backed into one of the stalls, and fastened with a halter and rope to each skelbrace. It would be left there for so many hours each day until it was decided if its 'mouth' was right and it would answer to the slighest pull by a rein on either side. The breaker had to be extremely careful that the horse's mouth did not get sore. As a good horsebreaker would say: "Give a horse a sore mouth and you have got a jibber."

He also kept chickens and sold the eggs. At that time they were twenty for a shilling. The wife bought some today at the local village shop and they cost sixty 'p' or, in the type of cash I know best, twelve shillings for one dozen, and as sure as not they would be from a battery of forlorn-looking things nearly unable to turn round. The only time they stand up is to drop their eggs. And if they miss a day or two, the next day is their last and they have probably never seen a nice grass paddock or scratted in a stackyard.

Grandma used to tell me to ask for eggs straight from the nest, because that meant you would get two dozen for your shilling, but you got them as collected — unwashed or cracked, you got the lot. I had also to ask for some chaff so that we could pack them safely into a bass for sending to Dad on the train. The Leeds train used to stop at our station in that distant past and Dad had an arrangement with the guard of a certain train to look out for me and collect the basket of eggs, then he met the train at Leeds.

I often wonder what some of those small farmers who keep a few chickens as a sideline for the wife's pocket money (usually used to buy his shirts or the children's clothes, only rarely spent on herself) would think of their descendents who have converted old nissen huts or built cheap draughty and cold sheds and installed row upon row of small wire cages, each with a poor imitation of those gregarious chickens that used to scratch about in the farm yard or the pasture, overlorded by a big old rooster whose main object in life was sex. He used to trot back into the hen party after it all and be bullied by an old hen that hadn't laid an egg for months because the family were keeping it for a special customer — a good fat hen was a good sale at Christmas.

The days passed quietly by: I loved my life, and Grandma spoiled me but was still firm about my goings and comings. Church was a must on Sunday, both morning and evening; slang words were forbidden, and all books except the Bible and "Uncle Tom's Cabin" were put into the cupboard. She was a bit straitlaced in her outlook. I think her parents had been comfortably off, because she and her brother and sister went to school when they had to pay to attend. She was therefore able to both read and write in an age when few of the working class could do so, and I can still remember her talking about the number of letters she used to write for the villagers.

She and Grandad had always kept a pig, and even after she was widowed she still kept one. It was an insurance against the doctor's bills, because many doctors in those days thought goods were sometimes better than cash, and a good ham well cured was worth a pound or two. She used to go gleaning in the fields nearby after each harvest, and I remember her lament that gleaning was not what it used to be before these new-fangled binders came on the scene and these new horserakes came and cleaned up the last few ears of corn. I think of her when I go across some of the corn fields today after the combine has passed over and see the spillage of corn that is left by some of the farmers in their hurry to get on with it. Even so the modern farmer produces more food per acre than his grandfather thought possible.

But Grandmother has gone and the cottager's pig has gone also. The days when a cottager could keep a pig in a sty as near to the back door as he wished vanished a number of years ago when the powers that be decreed that no pig-sty should be within a certain number of yards of the back door and that a pig should go to a proper slaughterhouse for killing. When I was a boy, our pig was always killed at the back door.

The brick-tiled yard was swilled, straw laid down, and the big copper in the washhouse put on. The big scalding-bath would have been soaking; it might not have been used since the last slaughter a year earlier, unless it had been used by one of the neighbours. The scrapers would be dug out of the cupboard. Two of the favourites were a pair of old pewter candlesticks. They lived on the mantelpiece, and Uncle Dick used to say they were not so hard on the pig's skin as they scraped the hair off the body.

The slaughterman would give his time of arrival beforehand, and sure enough would appear at the appointed time with his felling axe. The pig would be brought down from the sty, and everyone was full of excitement but trying to look unconcerned and remain quiet, as the bacon cured better if the animal was not upset or heated. A little bit of meal would be put in the straw, the slaughterman was at the ready and down would come the pole-axe. A second blow was never required. There was just a neat half-inch hole in the centre of the forehead, a quick withdrawal of his knife from its holder at his waist, a gash in the neck and the blood pouring out. Then the rest of the family got to work. One collected the blood in a bowl as it poured out, another changed the bowl as it filled and put the blood into a bucket where someone else kept it moving so that it did not congeal. That is how a perfect black pudding starts.

As soon as the bleeding stopped, the carcase was lifted into the scalding tub and the boiling — or near boiling — water poured over it, and the scrapers took over until all the hair had been removed. All was done at top speed before the body cooled, then it was taken into one of the sheds for the slaughterman to do the butchering part. All of them were journeymen butchers who worked for a master butcher two or three days a week and spent the rest of their time travelling the villages or farms. A good man at the job made a good living, and of course every job meant a piece of meat, which in the case of Harold, our slaughterman, was exchanged at the Bay Horse for beer.

The following day was cutting-up day, and back would come the slaughterman to cut the by now cooled pig into usable pieces, the two hams and the two shoulders and sides for salting and curing. As much as possible of the rest of the meat would be salted down, some of the intestines would be put into a bucket for washing and cleaning for black puddings, the bladder would be washed and cleaned for holding the rendered-down fat, which would keep it in perfect condition for a very long time. There would be plates of fry for the neighbours, pieces of chine and spare rib for married sons and daughters and the blood was used for black puddings.

The next job would be salting the hams and sides. It would be my job to fetch the salt from Elgey's, the chemist's shop in the Market Place, in those days a place where you could get nearly everything either for medical, physical or farm use. He sold salt in huge oblong lumps for pig curing or rock salt for cattle licks. Take your bottle and he would mix you a potion that would work wonders with the chap who complains "Ah nobbut feels queer at times Mr. Elgey." But it was a fascinating shop and even now that it has gone and a stately bank stands in its place, I can still see the portly figure with a seemingly permanent cigarette in his lips, standing at the shop door, and those marvellous aromas of bits of everything still seem to meet the nostrils.

The salt block would be crushed down and all the meat to be cured would have salt rubbed well into it and finally it would be left with a two inch covering, to soak into the flesh in due course. Usually the curing place was in the corner of the front room which nearly always had a brick tile floor, and many a new occupier of an old cottage that has been altered and modernised will often wonder why the corner in one of the rooms always seems to have a damp wall. Little do they know how many stones of salt have liquified in that corner and how much bacon and ham has been cured there. Nor can they imagine the hopes and wishes of the salters that they may this time be able to keep the whole lot and not have to sell it to pay some doctor's bill or cover the cost of one of the children missing being hired, which would mean having to keep them over the Winter until some farmer could give them a job. The pig was a godsend in years gone by and the new Health Act which stopped anyone keeping a pig within a certain distance of houses (I believe it was in 1912) caused an awful lot of despondency amongst the villagers.

CHAPTER THREE

1912 was also a landmark for the elderly. Until then old people past working life had a hard time unless they had a family that would help with an odd shilling or so each week to keep them off the starvation line, but in 1911 David Lloyd George introduced his National Insurance Bill which gave people of pensionable age five shillings a week — a godsend to millions. I can still remember Grandmother's joy on receiving her first pension. She was by then in her eighties and I fetched it from the post office for her. Uncle Dick had always been at home so his lodging money of ten shillings a week and the halfcrown that Dad was sending for my keep made her quite comfortable, except that Dick was flagman for a threshing machine engine and it was mostly Winter work. So during the Summer he was more often than not broke, so his bank was Grandma.

He was a tough chap, because he was sixty at that time and as flagman he had to carry the red flag whenever the threshing set moved from farm to farm and whenever horses were met he had to lead and steady those that shied at passing the smoking monster. He never learned to ride a bike, so he walked to wherever the machine had been set up. This was sometimes four to five miles away and meant leaving home in time to be on the farm at 7 a.m. in Winter and 6 a.m. in Summer. He then walked back after the day finished at 6 p.m. Grandmother never missed getting up and getting his breakfast ready and packing his lunch until the week before she died at 85. Long hours, but if you wanted a job in the country you had to put up with a bit of inconvenience. The workhouse was just round the corner and on the opposite side there was always someone ready to take your place.

Grandmother was born in 1830 and had watched the evolution of the threshing machine from the flail to the horse-driven machine which had a kind of turret with a shaft to which were yoked two to four horses depending on the type of corn being threshed and the speed required. The shaft went round and round in a circle of about twenty-five feet diameter and at the base of the turret turned a universal joint which coupled up with an iron shafting. This revolved and thus turned the wheel which worked the machine by a belt.

In those days the farm worker's wage was seven shillings a week. There were various improvements as the years went by, and finally the big people such as Ransomes, Marshalls, Clayton and Shuttleworth started to take a bigger interest in the project and finally turned out the big machines driven by a portable steam engine or by the big traction engine which we now only see driving the dynamos on the fairgrounds or as a curiosity at the local agricultural show, until they too were ousted by Mr. Ford and his tractors a hundred years later.

Driffield is now a thriving market town with various industries, particularly in the production of turkeys: One advert indeed proclaims: "You are now in turkey country." There is also a large factory producing clothing for national stores. But the two oil and cake mills are no more, killed by the modern methds of feeding stock on the farm. In the past the two mills, known locally as big and little mills, had all their linseed and cotton seed brought from the docks in Hull direct by barges to the canal head near the mills, where the seed was crushed and treated to extract the different oils and the residue mixed with other ingredients, one of which was crushed locust bean.

I can well remember the days when locust was being unloaded from the barges. The canal head was haunted by lads trying to grab the pieces that fell out of the baskets on their journey from the hold to the waiting cart. It was hard, tough stuff but it had a streak of sugar-like substance running through it, so we gobbled it. It is amazing what the human stomach can take, especially when young. The resultant product was heated and pressed into a slab about two feet by one foot and one inch thick. One was linseed cake, which had the higher feeding value, and the other was cotton-seed cake, used with turnips and chaff for feeding store cattle.

Up to a few years ago an incoming tenant to a farm paid a percentage of the outgoing farmer's bills for linseed cake over the past year, the reasons being that the foldyard manure was much richer from the linseed fed animals and was thus passed onto the land. Modern methods of feeding stock turns the foldyard straw into a compost with nothing near the old land value. One improvement, however, is that the modern cattle feed people make sure that what goes into the beast is used and not, as formerly, partly digested and the rest passed out.

With the closure of the mills the canal fell into disuse and what had been a glorious project in 1750 and had turned Driffield from a small village into a small town, fell into disuse in the 1920s. The final nail was hammered in when a concrete bridge was built at Wansford on the Wansford-Skerne road, an immovable object which only just allows the swans to pass under and which replaced the swing bridge. It is strange how a few people can similarly span a lot of years by reminiscences.

It is now 1984. Grandmother died in 1915, but I can remember her telling me that she was born in 1830 and that her grandfather told her that as a boy he went to work on the making of the canal and when it was finished in 1770 he could stand in Driffield Market Place and count every house in the town, and when the railway came (the Hull-Bridlington line was opened in 1847) Driffield became the centre of a large corn trade.

Incidentally, Grandma was present at the opening of the line. She told me that everyone had a holiday — she did not say whether they were paid, but I doubt it — and there were flags flying and lots of goings on. I suppose I must be one of the few people still alive who has talked to someone who was there and who in her turn had talked to someone who was at Driffield's other big event, the canal opening.

When we were on our own she often used to talk about the old days to me, just the same as we old ones now talk to the young ones if we can get them away from the television. But I am afraid that reminiscences are not for young folk, and yet this must be how a lot of our history and legends have been handed down through the ages before we had the "Daily Mail." When we think of three people spanning over two hundred years reminiscing about the past, what is a thousand years? Just a few more grandparents passing the action on to their grandchildren.

I wonder what our grandchildren will have to talk about to theirs? Everything seems so organised today. The papers seem to cover everything, there are no "odd bods" in the countryside as there were years ago, before authority got its hands on everything. But I will give credit for some of the things that progress has accomplished. Children all have the chance of a good education; the deaf and dumb that we were all too familiar with sixty years ago as well as the mentally retarded, who formerly became the village idiots, are now turned into useful members of society by finding suitable jobs for them. Even the hopeless cases with mental or physical infirmities get help and care that just a few years ago was unheard of.

The mental hospitals today are places that no-one should be frightened to go into for help and treatment, a very different kind of treatment from that which the inmates received in the days of the late 1800's that Aunt Polly used to talk about when she was home on her holidays from what in those days was called the Asylum. The inmates there were treated little better than cattle. Poor old Aunt Polly and Uncle MacCarty came back home retired in the 1920's. I can still hear her say: "My roots in Driffield are like an oak tree, they will take some uprooting." They both enjoyed their Guinness, and Uncle Mac — as nice an Irishman as ever breathed — drunk his last glass on the day he died. He had been a great campaigner and had medals to prove it and a host of stories to match them. I liked Uncle Mac.

One of Grandma's uncles was a carrier. He did a weekly run to Scarborough and the villages inbetween. I can hardly think of a worse run. The roads would be poor and more than likely rutted over the high Wolds, and in Wintertime he could be stuck for days, and the amount and depth of the snowdrifts at the top of Staxton Hill and Wold had to be seen to be believed. The only way at that time of clearing the road was by horse-drawn snowplough. This was a triangular-shaped implement made of heavy pieces of timber bolted together and pulled by four or more horses, depending on its size, which pushed the snow to each side.

But in Summertime it was lovely country. He did the run for many years, working it with a few acres of land in Driffield, but when the railway came and goods could go from Hull to Scarborough direct he gave it up. But there still remainded a lot of carriers with their carts or wagons. Most villages had one or more, and you could send a parcel from your own village to any part of the East Riding by giving it to your own carrier who would take it to the market town he visited with his cart and pass it on to a further carrier and so on, the original carrier paying for each transfer. The whole bill would probably be ninepence or a shilling.

Their charges were extremely cheap; even between the two wars my cash book shows Hull to Hessle fourpence, Ferriby and Preston sixpence, with Brough, Beverley and further parts of Holderness, one shilling. Then came the motor-van era, and most firms decided it was better to deliver their own goods. The customer was the loser, and the carrier disappeared, but the old carrier people still live on in a lot of the villages. They have adapted themselves and still rumble round the countryside with their huge lorries moving cattle, corn, or anything that can be moved.

The summers were passing and my days of playing and birdnesting were nearly over, but I can still remember the call of the corncrake, now practically an extinct bird, in that field in Spellowgate. With that instinct that boys have in the country, I would find its nest in the hedge-bottom with fourteen greyish brown spreckled eggs in it.

What a find, but it was a game bird and as such had to be left alone.

Spellowgate was also a stonebreaking centre where the stonebreaker plied his trade. The Council carter used to lead the large pieces of stone (granite) from the riverhead or from the station and tip it by the roadside in heaps. Then the breaker would apply his variety of hammers specially made for the job, ranging in weight from about a pound to four pounds. They had long ash-sapling shafts to give plenty of whip, and he would start off with the large size on the biggest lumps and change as they broke down.

It was, of course, piecework, so come rain you would see the stone-breakers working away with a bag over their shoulders. It was amazing how much water a sack would run off before it soaked through. In fact, most farm labourers always had a hired railway sack (the best on the market) with them in the fields on rainy days. But the breaker had to push on, and his heap had to show size before he could get a sub. Of course, one never sees those neat heaps nowadays. They were just two feet high with an exact slope at the sides so that the Highways foreman could measure exact the cubic contents of the heap and pay accordingly.

The stone when broken was used for road-making. All roads by now were macadam (tarmacadam was still a way off) and the procedure was that the steamroller pulled a heavy machine with four steel pointed bars which when lowered tore up the surface of the road to a depth of four to six inches. New stone was then spread on the top and a covering of mushy gravel, then it was well watered from a horse-drawn watercart. It was then ready for the steamroller to press the whole lot into a compact hard-surface road which in Summer raised clouds of dust when the new-fangled motor car came on the scene and produced puddles in Winter. Most cyclists carried a piece of pointed wood with them so as to be able to keep poking the mud out of their mudguards. They were aptly named were those mudguards! Oh, the bliss when the tarmacadam roads arrived.

As we travel the country roads nowadays we rarely see those brightly coloured fields of yellow ketlock or red poppies and that other pernicious weed, docking — not forgetting the thistle, which once upon a time was the sign of poor farming. With modern sprays they have all but disappeared, and with aeroplanes the spraying can be done at the right moment and they can release the spray within a few yards. So that, whether it be a ten-acre or a hundred-acre field, practically every square yard receives some of the liquid.

In the past, when our dykes and streams ran pure water, the only way to clear weeds was to pull them up, and that was usually a lad's job. So on Saturdays it was the job of one of the labourers who lived in the village or town such as Driffield to organise a gang of lads on the Friday evening. There would be about fifteen to twenty of us, aged about thirteen. If he had a few lads of his own, the average age dropped much lower.

On the Saturday morning we had to be at the farm by 6.15 a.m., and we were spread across the field, each with an area of two to three yards wide across the field; armed with a bag to collect the gatherings which were emptied out at each end. Just previous to 1914, the pay was ninepence a day. We finished at 5.30 p.m., then walked home, handed the money over and got a penny back for sweets. Farming hours were six to six, Saturday included.

Another get-rich-quick project, which was more of a job for the stronger lads turned thirteen, was carrying chaff and pulls on threshing days. It was the dirtiest and dustiest job on a farm. The chaff was blown out at the side of the threshing machine and the carrier raked it onto a sheet and carried it into the barn for cattle fodder. It was a hard and tiring job, and was paid one shilling and sixpence. The pulls were the screenings from the threshed straw and dropped out between the straw elevator and the machine. Moving them was another dirty job but not quite so heavy. The pay for the day for a lad was one shilling and threepence, and there was no keeping it all for yourself when you got home. It had to go into the "kitty" and you got a penny or maybe twopence to go out and spend as you wished after you had washed and got rid of all the dust and sweaty muck. There was none of the present-day "I've earned it and I'm keeping it." There was a belt always handy round somebody's waist and it would be used very quickly. Subordination was squashed very quickly. Every penny earned had to buy somebody something.

CHAPTER FOUR

The First World War had been on for some months now and finally I got my way and could go to work on a farm. Oh what joy to be able to go into the field and to be able to plough and harrow and sing the songs the men sung "And be a farmer's boy, oy, oy and be a farmer's boy." Little did I know that it was a trade, a very skilled trade, and I had a long way to go before I was master of most of it. It was, of course, the poorest paid trade of them all, but at that time a shilling seemed a lot of money and the thoughts of earning a shilling a day for six days a week was like the dreams of a contented banker, so I let it be known to all and sundry that I wanted a farm job.

It wasn't long before it turned up. One Saturday morning there was a knock at the door, and when I opened it there was a farmer we all knew as Sammy, wearing an old bowler hat which was greenish-black like his jacket and also fustian leggings. He never wore anything different, except in Winter he put on two overcoats and a woolly scarf. He was renowned for being very careful with his money. Some folks said that he was greedy, later on I called him a miser, but there he was at the door and his first words were: "I hear tell you want to work on a farm." I said I did. "Will you come and work for me?" "Yes." "How much do you want a week?" "A shilling a day, six bob a week."

Sammy stood back, "Good God lad, that's nearly a man's wage, I'll give thou five bob." "No," I said, "I've been working in Driffield for a chap for a shilling day." "Ay, that's the trouble these days," says Sammy, "Some of these townies will pay damn soft wages for onnybody. They've more money than sense." However, after a little more haggling he said: "Right, I'll give thou six bob a week and thou must be on the farm at six o'clock and work until six at night." I said: "Right I'll be there."

I must have done a bit of quick arithmetic because I added: "That's just twelve hours a day so that's just a penny an hour." Sammy jumped as though shot: "Don't thou talk like that my lad. Just think I lets thou have an hour off everyday for dinner and Saturday is a short day. All labourers knock off at five o'clock to come t'house for their wages and then they all go home. That's seven hours thou gets at me. I've a good mind to give thee only five bob." We both looked at each other, letting it sink in. Had I been a little "clever dick," I wondered, but he turned round and said: "Monday morning at six and don't be late." Elation, I was a working man, and so I was for another fifty-one years.

On Monday morning at six a.m. I was on the job with the other weekly labourers waiting for the foreman to give us our job for the day. Finally he reached me. "Now young un, what can thou do?" "Anything," I replied. "Um, that means thou can do nowt!" was the answer, "Go and help beastman until I find summat thou can do." So away I went, a bit disappointed because I was sure he would jump at the chance of sending me to plough, with the two best horses on the farm. Little did I know about the rigid structure of work on a farm and who did what.

However, I found the beastman, thank goodness. Old Bill welcomed me: "Yes lad, I'm sick of running after them bloody women at back door. It's Bill do this, do that, fetch this and that and chop sticks. Thou can do that. Can thou milk?" I said "No." "Oh, that's a bit awkward, but we'll soon larn thou; in the meantime get off to back door."

I knew which one, because the only door so termed on a farm was the back door at the "big house," the farmer's house. On a big farm no-one ever went to the front door. So I presented myself to the cook. "Oh," she remarked, "Bill's pushing his work onto you is he? Lazy old devil. However, get on with pumping up, the tank is nearly empty."

Before the arrival of the electric pump, or the arrival of electricity on the farm, the water supply for the big house had to be pumped by hand to the cistern in the roof from the well at the back door, and if there was a large family it was quite a big job pushing the pump handle forward and back, forward and back until the overflow started to run into the kitchen sink. Ah the sigh of relief when that first trickle appeared, after you had been pumping for an hour.

Another job was turning the milk separator. It was a newish gadget, they hadn't had it long. The old way of separating the cream from the milk was by pouring the milk into long shallow lead-lined troughs in the cellar and letting it settle for a day or two then skimming the cream off the top. The skimmed milk was then run off into buckets for farm use. But with the new way, you poured the milk into a large container on the top of the separator, turned a handle at the side, and the cream ran out of one pipe into a container and the skimmed milk into another one. Things were starting to move on the farm.

On the Saturday night at five o'clock four labourers and I waited at the back door for Sammy to bring our wages and then I got my first week's wages, six shillings. I know of no joy that can transcend the one of receiving and carrying home that first wage. I have received some good ones since then but I have never put it in my pocket and kept my hand there until I got home since that Saturday.

Grandma made a big fuss of me, and then when I had finished my tea and got washed, she gave me my pocket money, threepence, all for myself to spend as I wished. I had never spent threepence all at once so off I went into town. What a night out, spend it lad, so I did. First call, Star Supply stores, one of the forerunners of the big supermarkets, for a pennorth of boiled sweets, four ounces a penny, then straight across the road to the picture palace — another penny gone.

I remember the opening of the picture palace about 1912; before that the only moving pictures we saw were given by a travelling show which came to us in Driffield about twice a year. You sat on wooden forms right at the front for a penny, upstairs was tuppence, and it was threepence for the toffs on plush seats. Right at the back on a sloping platform it was standing room only for all the youngsters for a halfpenny. If I remember right, it was called Copland's Picture Land and at the front was one of the big old steam engines driving the dynamos and the musical instruments that played the tunes.

Before each performance there used to be a young woman who danced on the front platform to the music, she rattled a tambourine, and every now and then gave it a kick on a special note. Us lads thought she was marvellous. It was something to talk about for weeks. Then one day the place that had been a builder's yard had a big new building and a commissionaire who walked up and down in front of it proclaiming to all and sundry that this was the Victoria Electric Picture Palace, the home of animated pictures, seats at one penny, twopence and fourpence with musical interludes on the piano. So Aspland's pictureland came no more — progress again.

Two pennies were gone now — one to go. Easy, out of the picture palace, down the Market Place to the fish and chip shop. Mrs. Berryman's fish shop was a well-known emporium with a supper room, so my last penny bought me a ha'porth of fish and a ha'porth of chips, and they were no small portions of either. But oh, how I used to envy those chaps who could afford to go into the dining room. Granted, you sat on forms and the tables had oilcloth on them, but for threepence you got a plateful of fish and chips, vinegar and salt and a plate of bread and butter and a mug of tea. How I did long for the day when I would be earning a lot of money and I would be one of Mrs. Berryman's select customers.

Easy come, easy go, my money spent, plenty more where that came from next week. So home we went, my pal and I, the most contented couple in the town. Sunday morning we were always up bright and early. When breakfast was over, in popped Aunt Minnie. She lived in Hull and was married to a docker who was more out of work than in, and she seemed to have a permanent chip on her shoulder. Her first words were: "So you went out last night, didn't you, and spent all your money. I'm sure tuppence would have been enough for a lad your age and besides, you ought to start saving up for your clothes, you can't expect your Grandmother to buy them for you."

She was not my favourite aunt but I liked her husband, Uncle Fred. He was my favourite uncle. He was a keen Rugby League fan and used to go to the Tivoli in Hull and knew all the latest songs. Talk about two opposites, but they seemed to live in harmony. But to a lad of fourteen and a working man now, why worry!

I went into the cowhouse where Bill was busy milking. He was a good milker, fast, and the two streams of milk seemed to pour into the bucket without any effort. But when you have said that, you have given all his good points. I should have said he was a fast milker rather than a good one, because he was a wet milker and he never bothered to wash either his hands or the cow's udder before he started, and he chewed twist.

So far as hygiene was concerned it and Bill were strangers. Most women are, or were, dry milkers, and because so little hand-milking is done these days, the question of dry or wet milking does not arise. But the wet milker was wetting his hands continually in the stream of milk and the more he wet, the more the drips fell from his hands into the bucket and so on, and so on.

Bill was a bachelor, as were most beastmen in those days. They would start on the farm as ploughboys and work their way up. Most found that they were not strong enough to carry corn on threshing days, which was always the leading horsemen's job, or their feet let them down during the warm summertime. Sore feet were a penalty many farm hands suffered from during the Summer, walking day after day over hot rough soil with heavy boots on. On the other hand, some took the hot weather in their stride, their feet hardened off. But that was how often an unmarried man who wished to stay on the farm turned his hand to the foldyard and, like old Bill, stayed at the same place year after year.

Bill looked up: "Oh, it's thou is it?" I said: "Yes, I've finished feeding the calves and it's getting on for six o'clock." "Yes," replied Bill, "I was just thinking it's time thou started to milk these cows and then I could finish a bit earlier." "But I can't milk." "Oh, that's nowt, nobody can until they start. Get hold of that stool and get thyself under Old Jane there." He had by now finished milking Polly and was in his element: "Go on, get on her offside. Don't push her about. Get a bit nearer. Get the bucket underneath her."

By this time Jane was getting a little impatient, so she moved over another foot, and I had the whole business all over again. Finally I got myself fixed on my three-legged stool, hands at the ready. "Now lad," says Bill, "Get a good hold of them two front teats and pull 'em down and squeeze at the same time. Now you daft hound, squeeze finger and thumb fost and rest of fingers next." I struggled, but old Jane was holding back on me, a regular happening with a fresh milker. "Never mind," says Bill. By this time Jane was also getting a little weary of it all, so she stepped back about a foot, so that meant setting up a fresh position.

Suddenly her patience ran out, and wallop, she gave such a kick. When a cow kicks, it doesn't kick out and back, but inwards and upwards, and anything in its path as it brings its hind leg back is swept behind it and as it happened, that's where I was. It happened in seconds; one second and the bucket and me were on the floor, the next second I was flattened out in the muck channel behind her.

Bill burst out laughing as I got up covered in muck, tears of rage and pain from my disastrous episode with old Jane and screamed back at him. "Now, now," replied Bill, "look at her, she is laughing at thou, I've never seen her so content, I'm nobbut laughing at her, not thou." Still feeling sore, I remarked: "The old thing, she's that blooming scraggy she ought to be sent to the ket yard." "Yes," replied Bill, "but if thou gets as badly as she is, thou will be ready for the ket yard. She's badly lunged; she has TB that bad, we don't know whether she will hang out until the fellow from West Riding or somewhere out there comes for her. It's another month, but never mind, she's still giving a gallon of milk."

And that milk was going into human consumption either through the butter or to the lads as skimmed milk to drink at mealtimes. When we look at the standards demanded now by the Ministry of Agriculture we should be more than grateful for progress and the virtual elimination of that dreadful disease we once all lived in fear of.

Strangely, that finished my life as a beastman's lad, because the next morning the foreman met me as I walked on to the farm yard: "Hey lad, go with thoddy and fourthy scruffling and lead their horses." At last, amongst the horses — my first, to me, big moment. I would be leading two horses, one at each side of me, down the rows of turnips just showing in the rows, hardly big enough for the horses to see them, so that meant a leader until the turnips grew. The scrufflers were a metal framed contraption with one wheel at the front and two legs at the rear with a ten inch blade welded on to it. As the horse pulled it along, the blade cut the weeds between the turnip rows and, on a warm dry day, left the rows of turnips standing out ready for the hoemen to come and single them out with the weeds nicely dead.

Turnips were usually hoed or gapped by the labourers on piecework at so much per chain. If the labourer had a few children all the better, because he could then hoe faster by having one or two of the children following him, pulling all the extra plants out and leaving just the one plant for each gap that the hoer made. That was another daylight to dark job to make a few shillings extra and meant going hell for leather all the time — but that was the furthest from my mind. I was walking between two horses, me in one row and each of the others in another and the two men holding the scrufflers, one telling that the last lad that did my job was trampled into the hedge-bottom with the big chestnut Charlie, and the other one remarking casually that big Jack was a hand biter. He said that if he bit me while I was leading him I was to let him know at dinner-time and he would kick his backside.

This was my introduction — but not physically — to that most sadistic of the old farming ways of inflicting punishment on the 'youngest lad' by the seniors in the 'peck' order. Operated then by a kick from a heavy booted foot, it was supposed to keep the young lad 'in his place.' Used now, it would put the kicker in the right place, court. But at that time I was still a weekly paid lad and not hired.

CHAPTER FIVE

Harvest came and another lad had joined the army so I began to see less of the back door and was sent out with labourers first thing in the morning helping with the "opening out" of the cornfield. "Opening out" was done by one man or more, with a lad or — as often as not — his wife. He would cut by scythe a fifteen foot square just through the gate to allow the reaper to be brought into the field and be "set up" ready for the four horses to be yoked, two in front of two, and then he would start at the hedgeside and scythe a six foot breadth right round the field cutting from the hedge into the field.

With each sweep of the scythe he would carry the cut corn and, with a little tilt at the end of the cut, deposit the corn in a neat row, with all the heads pointing the same way, ready for the lad, or wife, to gather it up into sheaves. It was then tied up with straw bands made by gathering a handful of the cut corn, quickly splitting it into both hands, another split and a twist of the heads and then round the sheaf, the ends twisted together and tucked under the band. It would stand an awful lot of knocking about before it would come loose, and then it was leant against the hedge to be gathered up by the stookers.

I well remember the first time the conventional way of opening out by scythe was done away with on the farm I was on in 1917. It was the first field to be cut that harvest; extra labour was not available and on a thousand acre farm there was an awful lot of corn to be cut. "Right," said old Ted, the foreman, "Never mind what folks will say, I'm opening out from now on with the reaper. Get yoked up."

One of the labourers had cut the first few square yards for the reaper to get into the field and drive round the field the opposite way and cut the first swathe away from the hedge. Then, after the first round, he would go the proper way. So the first cut was round the field clockwise, throwing the sheaves into the uncut corn. This meant someone had to follow the reaper round moving the sheaves to the hedge side as they were thrown from the reaper.

The six foot breadth of cut left the way clear for the horses to travel on for the next cut and so on, going the correct way, which was anti-clockwise. It caused quite a commotion in the farming community, trampling good corn down and wasting the seed, said some. Doing away with the scythe men and good piecework said others. But within days every farmer round about was doing it and so they did until the combine harvester came to stay.

There was a lot of wet weather that harvest of 1915 and although we got the corn cut and stooked in the fields, it was difficult to get it led into the stackyard. The corn in the stooks began to sprout, particularly the wheat, and we would go into the fields in the early morning sunshine and turn the stooks over or re-stook them so they could dry after an hour or two, and by one o'clock it would be raining again. Wheat could be led when it was quite damp, but the stacks had not to be so big. Most farmers liked to build a stack that would take a full day's thrash. The foreman would measure out in the stackyard where the different stacks were going to be and their size when the corn was going to be led, knowing by experience that so many square feet of stack could go through the machine in a day. So if the corn was being led damp, the stack had not to be so wide, thus allowing the straw a chance to dry without going fusty and spoiling the quality of the grain.

Oats could be dealt with in much the same way. For one thing most oats were grown purely for feeding to the horses and beasts for fattening. So in a wet harvest one could see more long narrow stacks in the stackyard and quite often stacks in the fields, there not being enough room in the yard.

Barley was a different species altogether. It was usually the main crop, and in Wolds country the most valuable, most of it going for malting either to the breweries or to Scotland for whisky. So it had to be cut and harvested in the best condition possible, and usually in the Spring, when the young corn was just nicely through, a sowing of white clover — or seeds as it was known — would be sown; a set of light harrows and then a roller over the lot and the two crops grew up together. But if it was a wet summer the clover would grow to nearly the height of the barley, so that when the field was cut the sheaves contained a lot of green clover at the bottom. If this was not dried properly and was stacked in a damp condition it would heat and cause internal combustion and a resultant stack fire.

The most regularly used antidote to heating was to have chimneys in the stack. As it was being built, sacks filled with straw were stood at intervals on the base of the stack, and as it grew the sacks were pulled up a foot or two making a chimney from the base to the top and allowing any heat generated to get away more easily. They could be a bit of a nuisance when the stack was being threshed, for whilst not being wide enough for a man to fall into, when he was forking the sheaves to the machine, he could get a nasty twist if one leg slipped in.

Harvest was finally over, and the next job was the sowing of Winter wheat. This was always done on the previous year's clover or "seeds" fields that had fed the sheep and lambs during the Summer. The sheep had now been transferred to their Winter quarters, the sheep fold in the turnip field. Wheat was generally sown on the plough and press system. Three or four sets of ploughs, depending on the size of the drill, would start a rig on one side of the field and work round it.

The drill had three or four wheels so shaped that they pressed a groove about two inches wide between the tips of each furrow as they were turned over. Each plough was set so that it turned over a nine inch furrow, and the seed corn ran down from the box on the top of the drill in measured amounts down a metal tube to each of the grooves. By today's standards, the work was done at a snail's pace, but it all got done in its own time.

There were four ploughs, one seed press, and following up were two horses, one set of harrows covering seed up and me, driving my first pair of horses. Life, this was it; only one more ambition and that was to plough. But that was to be denied me for a few more weeks. The foreman told me: "Thou is too little," and that was that, but his son who was the same age as me: "Oh well, he's different. He's always been on a farm, and besides, thou's half a townie."

The weeks went by, the wheat sowing was over and November 23rd, Martinmas Day, arrived, when all the hired men finished their year's service and were paid the money due to them. What a super way of paying your labour, for a farmer. You hired your man, say the third lad, for twenty pounds plus his food for the year, Martinmas to Martinmas. He was allowed to sub, but never more than half of what he had earned, and if you had a dozen hired men, you got all your labour a year in advance, reducing as the weeks passed, before payday came.

In November 1915, Grandmother had taken to her bed. It had been brought downstairs into the front room; the staircase was a narrow, twisting one. She was eighty-four and her stout heart was having a struggle. Her last moment could come anytime. Father came over to see her and told me that he and Mother had parted and he would have to see what he could do about me, but first he would have to deal with my sister, who was a year younger than me. He had been gone home an hour when Grandma passed away. I loved her.

Aunt Jane and Aunt Alice were talking in the kitchen when I passed through into the yard. I had just got outside when one of them remarked: "What are we to do about him?" I had good hearing in those days. "Well," replied the other, "Jimmy says that he will look after him and let him learn French polishing with him." "Ah," replied the other, "I think he'll be better hired out, for if anything happens to Aunt Jane, there'll be both him and Jimmy with nobody to look after them. He'll be better off farming."

Martinmas week, Sammy paid me my six shillings and then said: "Look, Harry lad. I want to hire you for next year. How about it? I can't do with you any longer weekly, it's a bit awkward." Knowing my position, I said right, then Sammy, careful to the last penny, asked how much I wanted for the year. I replied seven pounds. "Good God, lad," he said, "that's an awful lot of money. I'll give you six." "No, I want seven. That's a first year off plough lad's wage." Sammy said: "Yes, but you're not a plough lad." "No," I replied, "but I would have been if the foreman had only let me have a go!" "Yes, but you were far too little!"

Then I got a long story about little lads and when I mentioned the foreman's son, was told, Oh, well, he was different. I said: "Well, I'll grow." "Maybe not," said Sammy. "You might be like one of them jockey fellows and never grow at all, and then what? I tell you what I'll do. I'll give you six pounds for the year, and if you are a good lad, I'll give you another ten shillings next Martinmas." I thought: "Oh, well, we've split the difference." "Right," he said, "Come back after your Grandma's funeral." I went out of the room, but if I had looked back, I am sure I would have seen a look of real contentment on his face. I couldn't see a year ahead, but Sammy could think a year ahead.

I reported in two nights later to the foreman's house which was to be my home for the next year. The foreman and the waggoner were still talking. "Now lad," was the greeting, "thou is hired now and things are going to be different. Thou has finished messing about at Gaffer's back door and larking with cook and that other lass. Thou has to do as thou is told either by me or my Wag here and not be cheeky to anybody or thou will feel their boot. Oh, and by the way, Wag's name is Harry, so from now on thou answers to Joe." I was hired; one step higher than a slave, but on the farm right at the bottom of the peck order.

The peck order started with the farmer, always known as the "Gaffer." Then there was the foreman, always called the "boss." After him came the head horseman or waggoner, sometimes worse to deal with than the boss. They varied an awful lot until you grew up and could hold your own. They were nearly always strongly built chaps, and on a large farm were able to dominate nearly everybody else. Next in line came the third man, then fourth. The wag had a lad to help him, known as wag's lad, then the fourth man had one, me. The shepherd and the beastman both had lads, and they and the groom answered to the gaffer only. There were a number of labourers. Some had cottages on the farm, and some lived in rented cottages round about. They answered to the foreman or the wag. Not even in the forces was the order more strict, but it worked.

That first morning I had to be up at five a.m., but that was nothing, I had been doing it for months. Then it was into the stables, brushing the horses until twenty to six, then in for breakfast. There were two bowls of cold water for the six or seven of us to wash our hands, then we went straight into the kitchen. The non-horse staff would already be sitting at one side of the long whitewood table waiting for wag to sit down; not a word was spoken.

The foreman would start to cut the beef. It was always cold beef for breakfast. Wag was served first, then in descending order to the last one, that first year, me. Breakfast was always a real filling meal of a good slice of beef, which was sometimes a bit fatty or gristly by the time the cuts reached the bottom of the table. Then there were always large platesize pies on the table. The biggest drawback to the meal was the speed with which it had to be eaten — usually ten minutes.

Wag was sometimes pushing his plate away before us young lads had got half our meat swallowed. That was how it went down: it was never chewed, and your piece of pie was forced down by copious drinks of tea which was usually served in a basin. It is amazing how long the human stomach can take such a battering but, except for the occasional belch, it did do. Never a word was spoken except for "Pass the pie please," if the pie currently being cut was near you.

One pie was always finished before another was started and I got my first lesson at that first meal on how to cut your piece of pie. The first cut was from the centre of the pie, the cutter holding the plate steady with two fingers on the pie to the right of the first cut. Then, without moving them he made his second cut to whatever size piece he wanted, to the right of his fingers. The next cut was about half an inch short of the centre, always anti-clockwise, so that the last piece of pie would have a hexagaon-shaped piece of the centre of the pie with it. Naturally this was the prize piece and sometimes to get it a chap would take a piece much larger than he would normally have taken, or somebody would gobble his last mouthful to get hold of the piece. But as one of the men said to me when I started to cut my first piece of pie: "Get thy mucky fingers off somebody else's piece." Sometimes fingers were not as clean as they should be and by cutting the pie by the farm method you only touched your own piece from the very first cut — not much but still an effort at hygiene.

Dinner was a more leisurely affair, taking sometimes fifteen minutes of concentrated gobbling of hot broth from a basin with a wooden spoon, then boiled beef and veg, and to finish off suet dumplings and treacle on the same plate. When you were hungry, you didn't notice trifles like that.

Every day there was a different meal at dinnertime, but every week was the same. A week's menu could be read: Sunday, roast beef and veg, Yorkshire pudding one inch thick with gravy or treacle, on the same plate; Monday, washday, same joint cold and veg, plum duff and custard (very thin); Tuesday, broth day with beef etc. — the beef, potatoes, turnip and dumplings were all boiled together in the copper. Sometimes the broth would be a bit thin and the lads would remark: "They didn't bother to empty the copper yesterday." Blazing hot day or cold, the menu went on. On Wednesday the beef would be roasted; Thursday we often got large bacon cakes; Friday a fresh piece of beef and veg and duff; Saturday a hash-up of everything. The two veg were always turnip and potatoes, or occasionally one of the large cattle cabbages would be an extra on broth days. At least it made the broth taste of something. Once dinner was over, we would dash back into the stables to get the chaff into the bins and the straw for bedding up at night.

CHAPTER SIX

Work finished at 6 p.m. The horses were stripped and given a feed, by which time it was ten past six, and we went across the yard for tea, or supper as it was always called. This was the last thing we had to eat or drink before breakfast the next morning. Again it was cold beef and pie, but this time it was always preceeded by ablutions for the night.

There were two bowls of water in the sink, sometimes warm. Wag and his lad had one, thirdy and fourthy the other. The young lads came next. Hands, face and neck were slopped over and dried on a wet towel. Then there was a leisurely fifteen minutes feed and back to the stable to clean and brush the horses and then bed them up. We finished about 7.30 p.m. and after that we could do as we liked. It was interesting to see how far some men would walk or, if they had a bike, ride for a glass of beer and a natter in their favourite pub, then back before locking up time. Some farms had a lock-up time of 10.00 p.m. Some left the door open at night, and one place I was at there was a lock but no key.

There were two kinds of foremen; one was the foreman pure and simple and on the smaller farms usually lived in one of the farm cottages with two or three hired men who fed in the farmer's house. The foreman who fed the hired men was known as a hind foreman. He was on the bigger farms and would have up to ten or more men living in. Of course, it rarely made any difference to him, but the work load on his wife was virtually slavery, particularly if he was the type who wasn't too keen to allow her to get the wife of one of the labourers to help her in the kitchen. And many of them brought up a family as well.

I lived in with one who had a family of eight girls and two boys, and there were twelve of us living in. A woman used to come and help her on washdays and baking days. In those days the only way that a man could hope to get his own farm, unless he was a single man and saved from his yearly wages for quite a few years, was to go hinding. The farmer paid from six to seven shillings a week for each man or boy — rarely seven shillings until the First War had been on a year or two and meat prices were moving up a little.

It was reckoned that each man ate one pound of meat per day, and the meat was bought once a week. If the farm was not too far from the village it would be delivered twice a week, but in hot weather with no fridges it sometimes got a big high. The farmer provided the beds and the bedding and that was all.

The men fed in the hind's house, which quite often backed onto the foldyard, and the men's bedrooms varied. During my first years at Sammy's we went to bed via the granary steps, through the woolroom where the fleeces were kept until sold. The bedroom contained five double beds, and that was all. There was no table; the only other things in the room were the boxes containing the men's own personal things and their extra clothes. Each box was the hired man's own property, ranging from small tin ones to the large chest type belonging to the older men which were sometimes passed down from generations.

The hind's wife came through a door each morning to make the beds and sweep out. Each man took his boots off at his bedside, having come straight from the stable, across the stackyard and through the barn. It was primitive, but then we were only the hired lads. On the other hand, if it was a smaller farm and the men lived in with the farmer the conditions could be very much different — a lot depended on the outlook of the farmer and his wife.

The farmers' or hinds' wives did no washing for the men. Usually the wife of one of the labourers would wash for those who were too far away from home to go each week with their shirt and socks. There were not many who wore vests and pants until they were married. The rates of pay varied, the usual one being a ton of coal bought from the station and tipped at the back door and fetched by horse and cart during Martinmas Week. You could get a ton of coal at the coal depot at the station for twelve to fifteen shillings. My first year off I paid Aunt Jane ten shillings for washing one shirt and one pair of socks weekly for the year.

All the men had three changes of clothes, one washing, one wearing and one in their box for wet days, the rule being that if it was raining before you were due to start work you waited until it faired up, but if you were in the fields you stayed out until you were wet through and that meant you were wet through to the skin. Then you went back to the farm, and by the time you had got the horses rubbed down and made comfortable, you put up with your own discomfort and let your clothes dry on your back. You can get used to anything; there's only one thing you can't do twice.

Back to that first morning. Once breakfast was over, we went into the stable and waited for the foreman to come in with the day's work. Bang on six, and in he came, always at the wag's end first, and worked down through the lads and then into the barn to give the labourers their jobs. The horsemen were going ploughing, then he turned to me: "Off thou goes to plough, Joe. Take Prince and Tinker. Get a move on and get their collars on."

At last a dream had come true. I was going to plough, but I said: "I can't plough. You said last week I was too little." "Yes, Joe," he replied, "but that was last week and thou is hired now, so shut up and get on with it!" I shut up. Both Prince and Tinker were eighteen hands, and I didn't reach fifteen and to put their collars on was beyond both my height and strength, so one of the others geared them for me and off we went to plough.

I walked on with the foreman's son to the field and remarked to him, "Funny isn't it? Last week I was too little to plough and this week I'm big enough." "Yes," he replied, "Sammy said to my Dad that he hadn't to let you plough before Martinmas otherwise he would have to pay you a ploughlad's wage and that would have been another ten bob for the year. Crafty old sod is Sammy; he hasn't hired me. I think my Dad's after a spot of his own at Lady Day, and he wants me to go with him and Wag's going to get married and he will be off as well." Never mind, I was going to plough and soon we would be at the field and I would be walking across it following my pair of horses and singing the songs that my forefathers had sung:

"Once I was a jolly ploughboy, ploughing in the fields all day,
When a very strange thought came into my mind
And I thought I would run away
So I've been and joined the army and I'm off tomorrow morn

(And then would come the chorus)
Hurrah for the Scarlet and the Blues
See our helmets glitter in the sun
Our bayonets flash like lightning to the beating of a military drum
For there is a flag in dear old England proudly waving in the sky
And the watchword of our soldiers is we will conquer or we'll die."

But I had reckoned without old Prince. Most farms in those days had one old horse, known as the old turnip horse, used by anybody for a carting job or fetching turnips in the Winter or nets and stakes for the shepherd, where speed didn't matter and the horse would be quite content to stand waiting all the day if necessary and they always had a "mouth" that you could pull at with the reins as hard as you liked and all it would do would be to swing its head to the particular side and go its own way.

Well, we had two of them and they were Prince and Tinker. What a combination to give a lad, nobody else would have taken them, but never mind, I would soon be singing, "Come Prince lad, you on the near side, Tinker in the furrow." He wasn't quite so bad on his feet as Prince and a bit lighter legged. Wag came across to me: "Don't overdo them two hosses," he remarked. "Thou had better go to that other rig and plough there. I don't like them two breathing down my neck all the time."

I was some time before I appreciated his humour. One of Prince's failings were greasy legs, a failing amongst all Shires if they were not attended to regularly. They suffered from a condition which made the legs itch, and if they came in contact with any of the gears or chains they would rub like mad until you could persuade them by "heavy methods" that it was more comfortable for them to move. Prince and the rest of them would play havoc. Yoking was soon done, it was nothing fresh. The moment had arrived: "Gee up Prince, come on Tinker."

It was ten yards to the end of the row. The others had set off and were turning round on the headland to go down the next furrow. All was well. "Woav up Prince." "Woav up" was the term used for calling a horse to turn to the left, and "Gee back" for a right turn. "Woav up Prince." We were leaving the others to go higher up the field. Prince didn't hear me. "Woav up," I yelled and pulled the rein. Prince affected not to hear. "Blooming kid, trying to push us around Tinker lad. Come on, let's teach him some horse sense."

The two of them turned gee back to follow the others, then the traces caught on Prince's hind leg. It wouldn't have happened with an experienced ploughman, but it did happen, and Prince was in heaven, rubbing his legs on the trace, almost sitting down to it in his ecstasy, and I knew that if he wasn't stopped quickly he would rub and keep backing until he reached the plough and then there would be proper trouble.

I yelled for Bob. He was following me up and grabbed the reins, which were always called strings. They were a quarter inch cord and stretched from the bit to the driver behind the plough. When wielded by an experienced man they could be made to act like a whiplash, and with each slash from the full length they would leave a wheal the full length of the horse's flanks.

Two quick strokes and Prince very quickly forgot his itchy legs and shot forward in response to Bob's shout of "Giddup there. Keep the old beggars moving at the ends and use them strings on him if he gets a bit out of hand. Thou will soon learn how to make him feel it." He was a crafty old blighter and knew all the tricks of the trade. Put too big a load on the cart he was pulling and he would jib and nothing would make him move until most of it had been unloaded. He was more stubborn than a mule (and I have driven some of those).

If it was a fine morning when I fetched the horses up from the pasture at five o'clock, Prince would be at the gate waiting. But be it a cold wet one, and you could bet that he would be sheltering by the plantation at the bottom of the dale. Poor old Prince, he used to "boss" all the rest of the horses: the peck order is just as strong amongst the animals. But in 1916 some army horses belonging to a party of soldiers who were baling a clover stack in the stackyard that Sammy had sold to the authorities and had been turned out into the small paddock, along with Prince and a mare and foal, must have taken a dislike to him, because one of them kicked him and broke his thigh.

Poor old Prince; the fellmonger came with his cart and took him away. I always used to think it was most undignified for a horse, which in its prime had been one of the most dignified of all animals, to be either shot or poleaxed and then winched by the neck onto the special cart that the fellmongers used, then covered with a couple of bags and taken away. I don't think Sammy worried about him because for a horse eighteen hands high, sound in wind and limb and a well-bred Shire, he claimed the price for a good working horse which at that time was about £50.

At last knocking off time came and I had got through the day with just one or two more do's with Prince and Tinker, but the plough was heavy and with me being a lightweight I hadn't done much singing and it was "homeward plods the ploughman on his weary way!"

I still had to get the knack of grasping the horse's collar with one hand and the end of the mane on the top of the withers with the other and springing on to its back belly down and a quick roll over to be sitting sideways on its back. No-one every rode a horse astride — this was the quickest way to get a sore bottom — so until I could do it with my own height it meant leading the nearside horse to a convenient object high enough to start my jump.

We finally got into the stables and I took the collars and traces off my two and was standing wondering what to do next when the foreman passed by. "Now then, Joe, what is thou doing?" I replied: "Nothing." "Oh well, we'll see to that right away. Go across to Bob's stable and tell him I've sent thou to be his lad and do all his work for him."

By this time it was ten past six and supper time, so off we went into the foreman's (hind's) house. Once supper was over, I made my way back to the stable with Bob. The foreman had told him that I was to be his lad, to feed and clean the horses for another hour, then bed down for the night. By this time I was so tired that when I had finished brushing I leant against the stable wall and fell asleep standing up. Bob howled, he thought it a great joke. "Never seen a fellow go to sleep on his hind legs. Heard tell of them on a clothes line but never seen this before. Better get thyself off to bed."

CHAPTER SEVEN

Bob was probably the nicest chap I ever worked with, maybe because he was nice to me when all around couldn't care less or were downright indifferent to a first-year-off youngster. He was of medium height, well built, with a heavy moustache, and he only shaved once a week. He had a ruddy complexion and by the weekend he looked a real villain.

I used to think that he was an old man of sixty or more, but after I left Sammy's I didn't see him again until the end of the Second World War almost thirty years later when I drove an ambulance during the Blitz and took someone from Hull to the Driffield hospital and Bob opened the gate to let me in.

After getting rid of my patients I went looking for him and in the course of our conversation he told me that through his lameness he couldn't work and he was now sixty-five. He was an inmate of the workhouse attached to the hospital, and as he could do nothing else he was temporary gatekeeper. We had quite a little natter, and as I was going he said: "I still likes a pint when I can get one Joe lad. Has thou got a couple of bob thou doesn't want!"

I was happy to give him what silver I had in my pocket. The next time I went I enquired after him and they told me he had died. I still remember Bob when I have forgotten a lot of the other chaps I worked with. We often used to sit on the cornbin top after we had finished the horses and talk. I think we both liked to talk and I was a good listener when Bob started to talk about bygone days and places he had worked at and things he had done.

He was lame and one of his feet was quite deformed. I said to him one day: "I say, Bob, how did that happen, that funny foot?" "Why," he said, "I'll tell thou. Dost thou know, I had the best two years of my life through that foot. Yes, I was up at Walkers up at Wold Top, I was wag there. I'd only been there a few weeks and me and the Boss were fetching a load of turnips from the field. We had got loaded and I was just jumping on the front of the cart to drive back when when the Boss said: 'Gee up Polly.' The mare shot forward and I fell off the shafts and the wheel went over my ankle and squashed it in the mud. A right old mess it made of it.

"When we got to hospital the following day, the Doctor wanted to cut it off. He said it was hanging off and that was all they could do, but I said 'No, God put that foot on and if he had wanted it off, cartwheel would have done it. He wouldn't want anybody else to do the job for him!' However, I was laid on my back for months and at last it set like this and it's a lot better than having a peg leg.

"Anyway," said Bob, "just a year after it happened I got my compensation, a hundred pounds. That was a lot of money lad; many a fellow has started off farming with that lot." I said: "Yes Bob, have you still got it?" "Naw," was the reply, "I told thou about that two years — well I put it in the bank and every Saturday morning I used to go and draw out one pound, never more, and I used to go back to my lodgings. I was with old Sep Smith and his wife. I put the bank book back in my box, paid the old lady eleven shillings for my board — I always gave her a bob a week more, 'cause it was a good spot — then I used to go to the little Red Lion and give landlady six shillings. That paid for five pints of ale a day for six days; it was tuppence halfpenny a pint then and if you put a bob down you got five pints for it, one pint afore dinner, two after it and two at night.

"I lived like a lord Joe lad." "But what about Sundays," I asked. "Oh I was all right on Sundays. Thou knows little Red Lion only had a six day licence and I always went to Chapel on Sundays and you gets used to one beer, but if I wanted a pint or two I could go to big Red Lion — same beer, but theirs was from pump and I preferred tap."

"What about the rest of your pound?" I queried. "Well, I had to buy clothes and boots and things, and there was always somebody hardup cadging a pint. But it all went, and I never drew more than my pound a week from the bank. Then one day the chap at the bank said to me: "Well, Bob, you have just one full pound left in your book and a few shillings interest. Are you leaving it in?" I says: "No thank you, I'll take the lot now and make it last a fortnight, then I'll go back to farming if I can get a job.

"However, I went to see them up at 'Wold' where I had my accident and he told me I could start again on Monday but it would be work for my keep until I got used to work again and said: 'Besides, with a groggy foot, thou may be no good at all!' But I had to do something and there was a lot of chaps out of work, so I went back but after a few months the old man didn't want to give me any money except an odd shilling or two, so I said to him: 'Look here Master, I can't go on like this,' so he says to me: 'Right, Bob, we'll part company and thou can go somewhere else if thou can.'

"So I left and came here to Sammy. He doesn't pay me as much as the others but he gives me enough to live on so I doesn't grumble. Besides, it's no use, and when I can't work, I'll go up the road to the workhouse. They will look after me." Poor old Bob; that is where he finished, but even to the last I bet he would still have many a quiet smile over those two that he called "the best two years of his life."

The Winter of 1915/16 was a hard one. Snow, slush, frost, we had it all, and I had chilblains on my hands and feet. My boots were getting a bit tight for me and the chilblains were making them worse and first thing in the mornings my miseries were complete when I tried to push swollen feet into tight heavy boots. Oh, the agony. The man who invented those rubber wellingtons deserves one field on every farm named after him if only for the discomfort he has saved country men suffering from chilblains and wet feet walking across fields and muddy tracks.

Another call that I dreaded that first Winter was the foreman shouting: "Hey Joe, get a couple of horses yoked into a wagon and get some straw into the foldyards." It would be a wet or snowy morning, too wet to go ploughing, so until it faired up, it was yoke the two horses into a wagon, with everything cold and wet and still not daylight, and pull it alongside the strawstack. I would be standing on the wagon ready to level the straw as it was thrown down to me.

'Wag' and 'thoddy' would put the ladder to the stack, climb up, and without fail would drop a forkful of wet straw and snow on my head. Then the shout would come: "Sorry Joe, didn't know you'd arrived!" Sadistic brutes. Sympathy was a thing they kept for their horses, never for a fourteen-year-old lad.

I well remember an incident that Winter. Every morning the horses were led out to the pond just outside the foldyard gates in the paddock for a drink in fine weather, but when it was wet we opened the gates and turned them loose one at a time to go for a drink, knowing full well that they would go straight back to the comfort of the stable. But this particular morning I had opened the gates and my poor feet were stuck in a sea of mud and muck when Bob let Bewlah loose for his drink.

Bewlah was probably the biggest horse I ever had anything to do with, over eighteen hands and a full ton in weight. He came thundering across the foldyard straight towards me. I panicked and tried to jump out of the way, but my feet remained glued in the muck. I shouted and then waved my cap at him, but my visions of being trampled to death in the foldyard muck were about to be realised when he eased up and trotted past me. Bob stood at the stable door and laughed but I had learnt how to swear by then!

Bewlah was Bob's pride and joy. He told me that he had never had one like him before. His skin shone not only with brushing but with sheer good health and good feeding as did the other three that the two of us looked after, Daisy, Polly and Tom, each with their own ways and peculiarities. Tom was a rascal. If he had been a human he would have been another Bob. Daisy was as quiet as an old sheep, with a gentle mouth and fat as butter. As time went on, Sammy decided that his hackneys were too risky for him to drive in the trap to market, so each Market Day Daisy was squeezed between the shafts and the two of them meandered their way to town.

Just around that time Sammy seemed to have a phobia about dying. He wouldn't take a risk with animal or weather. If it was wet, he didn't turn out, and in Winter he put overcoat on top of overcoat and never came out without his fustian leggings on and his billycock hat and he never walked across the foldyard. Not that that was a wise thing to do at any time, because he had the nastiest tempered bull I've met, a shorthorn, that would stand in the foldyard bellowing and snorting and he loved to get his horns under the tumbrils and turn them over and over if he was in one of his moods at feeding time.

He would calm down a little to allow Bill, the beastman, to put his scuttles of cut turnips into the cribs, but when he went to straighten the upturned tumbrils Bill always carried a pitchfork, the only thing the bull was frightened of. Some of the horsemen used to scrape him down his flanks with their forks if he came near them when we were leading straw into the yard. It was a savage tool if the points were sharp.

I once saw him in a complete state of impotence though. All the manure had been led out of the foldyard and piled up just outside the gates and Fred (that was what we called the bull) loved to amble up to the heap, walk into it a few feet throwing the muck all ways with his horns. But this time he ventured a little too far in his excitement. The ground sloped a little just there, it was similar to a pond hole, and Fred got beyond his depth and the more he struggled and bellowed the worse he got until the noise was heard by one of the men who went to investigate.

By then Fred was in a state of exhaustion so we had to fetch old Prince, the only one of the horses that wouldn't shy if Fred came out rushing. Prince had a set of chains put on and a couple of ropes fastened to them and, after a struggle, round Fred's neck and tied. It was then: "Gee up

Prince," and a slow gentle pull, and out slithered Fred, completely exhausted and blowing, with hardly a limb moving. He was completely beat.

However, after a short time he struggled to his feet and after a pat or two for his pluck, something he had probably not had before, and after a rub-down by Bill with a few handfuls of straw he wandered back into the paddock never to be seen near the muckhill again. Strange though, but if it had been a horse in the same predicament it would have died. It is a fact that a beast that is ill will lie down quietly and suffer and then after a rest get better, whereas a horse with the same or similar complaint would be thrashing about the place. Even a case of colic or bellyache can be serious, and if the vet is not called it could die. A good horseman had to know more than just "Gee up, Prince."

CHAPTER EIGHT

It had now got into 1916 and our foreman, who had been looking for a small farm of his own, finally decided that he had got enough cash and took an eighty acre place, so he and his son left us. As he had been the hind as well it left Sammy rather awkwardly placed without a hind and nine or ten of us to be fed. So we all had to get our meals in the big house, and the wife of one of the labourers came in daily and tidied up our bedroom and they got another maid in the house.

We had had good food in the hind's house but in the Master's house it was really good. This was quite understandable in a way because the hind was paid the minimum amount per man and he was hinding to make more money. If he was ambitious to own his own place he had to make his money out of his men. But on the other hand if he cut the food to them, nothing travelled faster than the news that so-and-so kept a poor table. At hiring time he would have a job to get labour on the farm and most good men would refuse to hire. Times would have to be very hard for him to get a full set of lads. It reacted in the same way with the farmer. His place got a bad name also which could last for a year or two. So if his hind left and he could not be replaced quickly, he had to feed the men and as he wanted to keep a good name for feeding it was nearly always tip top, so in we went.

Sammy was a bachelor, so his sister acted as housekeeper and cook for him. I can still picture her: she was a well-built young woman, fresh faced, and always seemed to have a smile. The wagoner on the place was courting her, and within a month or so they both left us to start hinding themselves. A very efficient pair they made too. I remember them a few years later taking a small farm of their own near Bridlington.

Cook was super, but the other girl — or lass as the youngsters were always known — would be fifteen, just a few months older than me, and couldn't even boil the kettle properly. Each morning we got a basin of tea with a breakfast of beef and fruit pies, and each morning she would get up at the last minute. It was nothing for her to lie in bed until half past five, then she would rush round, soak the firewood in paraffin and pile it under and round the big old cauldron. She would get the thing so hot and the handle the same and then she couldn't lift the cauldron off the fire, so she had to lift the lid off with the fire tongs and ladle the boiling water into the tea pots. In the meantime the smoke was belching into the top so that morning we got smoked smelly tea.

We never knew which was worse, that, or when she was on what we used to call her late shift, her five-thirty get-up. She was supposed to be up at five prompt, and as we lads came in for breakfast at five-forty, a late get-up meant that the water never did boil and until the last moment she would be lifting the lid every few minutes to see if it was boiling. At the last moment, as we came into the kitchen, the water would be put into the teapot, so we got smoked tea that wasn't mashed and half cold with the tea leaves floating on the top so that each mouthful was preceded by a blow to puff the tea leaves to one side.

For our tea, or supper as it was always called, it was a basin of skimmed milk or skilly as we named it. Every other night we had the same procedure — rush in, big fire, pan of milk on, so we got burnt milk. What a lass she was, but she got on well with us all, a happy-go-lucky type.

She was the first girl who ever tried to seduce me — it was in the barn one evening. We met and talked as youngsters do, when suddenly she grabbed me and told me how she loved me and would I, etc., etc. But even at that age I had seen what happend when two animals had sex, and besides at that age I was only just starting to grow up, so I refused! She must not have been too put off by it because a year or two later I heard that she had got her first baby and marriage was still a long way off, and by that time I had met her sister and much preferred her!

But living in with Sammy suited us all, and good food makes good workers. I sometimes wonder if half our modern troubles stem from the fact that half the workers are not properly fed.

Threshing days were the days that I detested most of all. Getting everything ready was far beyond me. The old portable engine weighing near on five tons had to be dragged from its resting place in the stackyard and set up near the next stack for threshing. The same three horses were used; Jack and Charlie in traces in front and Jenny in the shafts, as near three tons of horseflesh as makes no difference.

It was noticeable that when the foreman walked into the stable to give orders out, as soon as moving the machine was mentioned and the two pairs of heavy link taces were reached from their hooks, both Jack and Charlie, who had the same double stall in the stable, immediately stopped eating and stood back from the crib and were as tense and excited as any prima donnas before a big show. It seemed as if they knew that this was their big show, which, indeed, it was.

None of them had ever been known to jib, and that five tons sometimes took some moving in Winter time when the stackyard floor was not as hard as it could be. Yoking them up to the engine was the worst job. All three horses were excited, and foreman, wag and thoddy were trying to calm them down and getting themselves into a tizzy also. When they had finally got them yoked it was "Bellies to the ground," as we used to say. With a heck of a heave the engine was moving and then finally resting in its place.

Then the bigger but not so heavy machine that did all the threshing had to be brought alongside the stack, not too near, not too far, just right was near enough. Then the straw elevator had to be put in position at the end of the machine to catch the straw as it dropped from the machine. The last job was making sure that all the three were level, so then old Charlie, the blacksmith, who always drove the engine, brought out his spirit level and the lifting jacks, six to eight foot long ash poles squared off to five inches square at one end with a heavy steel slightly curved tip bolted on. With those two men could lift any weight by leverage, whilst packing was put under the wheels to make everything level. In the meantime, the horses were taken back into the stable to calm down and were given a feed.

The following morning before it was daylight, it was everybody to their job. Everybody knew their job: it was a ritual. Wag and thoddy would be carrying the corn from the machine into the granary, and fourth lad would be on the strawstack with one other helping him. There were two men on the corn stack forking the sheaves to two men on the machine, one cutting bands fastening the sheaves and the other feeding the machine putting each sheaf into the spinning drum in the correct way depending on the type of corn being threshed.

If one went into the drum without having the band cut, which did happen occasionally, off would come the big driving belt from the engine to the machine, to much swearing from the foreman and sighs of relief from everyone else for a few minutes rest until the belt was replaced and the drum released. The biggest sighs of relief would come from the two youngest members of the team, myself and the other young lad, for our job was carrying the chaff and the pulls.

The threshing machine did five jobs: the corn came out at one end and dropped into bags fixed ready for it, the straw at the other end dropped into the elevator and away it went, the weed seeds and bad corn were riddled from the good and came out of a separate exit, but the chaff and the dust and muck dropped on the floor between the stack and the machine, and the "pulls," which was all the riddling of the straw, dropped between the elevator and the machine and had to be raked out from the narrow space between them.

Both the chaff and the pulls had to be carried to the barn and put in separate heaps for feeding horses and cattle. We used sheets about six feet square for carrying it, laying the sheet down on the floor, if there was room. If they had "set" the machine too near the stack, there was not enough room to do it, so one had to manage the best way possible. It was the dirtiest job imaginable and it was always supposed to be a lad's job. Grown men wouldn't do it, but then when I was at school some of us used to go to the local farms carrying chaff — which was the heavier work — for one and sixpence and carrying pulls for a shilling a day. There was no arguing; if you wanted some extra money you did it and if you were hired you had to do it, it was as plain as that.

If a man was strong enough, the best job on threshing day was carrying the corn as it came from the machine. It was a regular but not a rush job and each of the two carriers took alternate bags. The corn bags were a standard size and were always filled to the top, just allowing for it to be either tied up or folded over so that the carrier held the folded flap whilst he was carrying it up the granary steps to be emptied on the floor.

Beans and peas were carried at twenty stones, wheat at eighteen, barley at sixteen and oats at twelve to the bag. Many a young lad has ruined his back muscles for life by trying to, or being made to, carry corn before he was strong enough. Wherever farm men met one could see the results of it, misshaped backs and shoulders. It was a job I did but once. I carried oats at one farm, but at dinnertime I told the foreman that I was doing it no more because I wasn't strong enough. I never did so again through my farming life and now, at eighty, my back is as straight as it ever was.

For many years there had been a body of men known as the Wolds Rangers who were for the most part ex-army men who had served varying terms of service in the forces and on discharge had drifted back to their old haunts but could not settle down to the humdrum of a six a.m. to six p.m. working day. So they roamed the Yorkshire Wolds from its start at the Humber to its precipitous finish at Flamborough. They wandered from farm to farm doing any kind of job on the farm for a shilling or two and their food. Then off they went, living rough in Summer outside and in Winter wherever they could get shelter. Most farmers tolerated them as a source of casual labour and would let them doss for a few nights in the shed, never in the barn or stackyard as they were all inveterate smokers and after a few pints at the local their habits became rather careless. A lot of them had small pensions or reservists pay, and when that came through there was no work until it was finished.

They would move to the nearest market town to one of the common lodging houses. Every town had two or three in those days. The inmates paid a few coppers a night for a bed and a right to sit at a table to eat whatever food he brought in and a place at the communal fireside. If he made a nuisance of himself, the lodging house keeper could call the police, with whom he was licensed, and he had the right to enter at any time to check any person he was suspicious of and have him evicted. This made things rather awkward for his future, as he would be black-listed and known trouble-makers were refused entry at most of the better lodging houses.

Conditions were rough at all of them, but some were better than others and they served a purpose for those who just had a few shillings a week and did not want to go into the workhouse or for such as the Wold Rangers, who wanted a home during the worst of the Winter weather. Nowadays, under the welfare state, no-one need go hungry or homeless.

The outbreak of war in 1914 claimed a lot of the Wold Rangers back into the forces, and the direction of labour during the war years forced those who were unfit for the forces into regular jobs. Thus ended a body of men who had roamed the Wolds for generations, a happy-go-lucky breed who were always ready to tell a story of their army days and the countries they had visited.

Such a one was Soldier Bob, who had put roots down at Sammy's for a considerable time. He had dug a trench about ten feet long and two feet wide in the horse pasture and lived and slept in it with a young woman who was very obviously pregnant when she first came to the dugout. As I was a regular visitor and at the time and age very innocent of the ways and means of people, I asked Bob one day what would happen when his wife had her baby and where she would put it.

"Oh, that's all right," replied Bob. "That is quite all right. She will go to stay with her parents, but by the way my boy, she is not my wife. I am just looking after her until she finds a nice kind husband. I am far too old for her. I am now forty-five and I may go back into the army. I was a sergeant in the light infantry you know." "Yes," I replied, "Yes, but where do her parents live?" "In Driffield, my boy," he said, quite airily. "Mother lives in the biggest house on Bridlington road, her father goes away quite a lot."

My brain did a quick journey up the Bridlington road and the few houses in it, only about a dozen. "Is that right?" I asked. "There are some big houses on there and I know most of the people that live in them." "Oh yes," was the answer, "but you quite evidently don't know everybody because it's quite true what I am telling you, the biggest but not the best on the road."

Even then the penny did not drop and it wasn't until I was telling Bob in the stable all about it and he said: "Why, you softhead, he means the workhouse. It's the biggest but not the best on the road and her mother goes there when her father gets pinched for poaching or suchlike. He's never done a good day's work in his life and his lass is taking after him. She is just the type for Soldier Bob. She will finish up in the grubber with a gang of kids and Soldier Bob will go into the army and never come back this way again." And that was how it all worked out. But I liked Soldier Bob; he was the first man who ever told me about another world and treated me as a pal. I will always remember his Captain Kettle ginger beard and his quick infantry walk.

CHAPTER NINE

Our waggoner had left us to get married and it was now Lady Day, the time in the farming world for leaving and selling farms. Hired men could leave the farm or stay with the new tenant or owner. Westfield Farm had been sold and Sammy got one of their men to come to work with us as wag and bring his young brother with him as his lad. What a pair. The older one turned out to be the nastiest piece of work I have ever worked with. It was his first year as a wag and it was just too much for him. One of the labourers had been acting as foreman until we got another hind, but old Jeff was pushed to one side by this brash pugnacious youth who was just starting to feel his feet.

Myself, I was a victim right from the start when he told me: "Our kid is above thou, and thou mind what thou does or I will kick thy backside" — a threat he carried out one day when it was raining heavily and he had told me to sweep up the stackyard. Everyone else was under cover and I grumbled to one of the others about it when suddenly there was such a kick at my bottom that I thought had broken my pelvic bone. I walked lame for some time afterwards. "There you young sod. Take that and in future when I give thou a job to do, do it without muttering," was wag's remark.

I hated him from that moment. Hate is the most powerful anti-social feeling of all. I could happily have murdered him. I spent hours thinking how I could get my own back; a gun was out of the question and I was too young for anything else. I had no big brother, and it would be years before I was big enough to tackle him myself. But oh, how I promised myself that one day I would get my own back. But it never happened. He finally went into the army and our ways never crossed again. But that was a way of life in those days, and nobody interfered with the wag. He was the boss and that was it. But every Martinmas at the various hirings, there were always a number of fights in the pub yards between some wag and one of the lads he had at some time punched or otherwise ill-treated, who had now grown up and got the strength necessary to "get his own back."

But the power of the wags was coming to an end. A few years later with the war over and a more enlightened workforce and the power of the then emerging farm workers union to back the lad in a prosecution, the power of the boot went out, thank goodness. However, that was some years ahead, and I was still under a sadistic wag, but I had got a champion. Usually the ways of what was termed "squaring the young lads up" by the wag was commented on by the rest of the men but rarely questioned. But this time, incensed by my condition after the brutal kick and the quiet content of the kicker, Tom the third lad, next to the wag in seniority, burst out.

Tom was a big tough lad. He came from Nornabell Street in Hull, a tough working class district, and he had been used to looking after himself all his life and could use his fists on with the best of them. He told wag in my hearing that if he didn't stop, as he put it, clouting and bunching that lad, he would chuck him down the granary steps and shove him through the rolling mill. Wag, the miserable slug, backed down, so at last I was free from physical threat. By the time Tom joined the army, we had got a foreman who could control wag and keep him in his place. I made enquiries about Tom when I eventually went to work in Hull but he was one of the unfortunates who didn't come back. I was sorry. I would have liked to have met him as an adult when I was able to look after myself physically, to thank him. He proved that "a bully and his courage are soon parted."

I was not all despondent. I had been told to expect a certain amount of bullying but not to worry, I would grow up in time. And my poor feet had at last parted with their chilblains and my boots fitted me once again and my voice could he heard across the fields singing one or another of the old songs:

'Said a pale-faced boy to his loving Mother,
    Let me cross the wide wide sea,
For they tell me that in a foreign country
    There is health and wealth for me.
So the Mother listened with fond affection,
    Though her heart for him did yearn,
And she sent him forth with a Mother's blessing
    On the ship that never returned
No, it never returned, No, it never returned
    And its fate is still unlearned
And from that day to this, they have been watching and waiting
    For the ship that never returned.'
"Gee up, Tinker; wake up there, Shot," then out would come the next verse:

'Only one more bag of the golden treasure
   Said the sailor as he kissed his fond young wife
Only one more bag of the golden treasure
   Then we will settle down for life
Yes, we will leave this shack for a little cottage
   And enjoy the wealth we've earned
So she sent him forth with a lover's blessing
   On the ship that never returned
No, it never returned, No, it never returned
   And its fate is still unlearned.
And from that day to this they have been watching and waiting
   For the ship that never returned.'

Lovely old melodrama, but we were now being flooded with dozens of new wartime songs, and it was amazing how quickly they reached even the most remote farms. There was no wireless and television was still a dream, but copyright on songs was another thing to come, so papers or anyone who cared to put a song and music on a piece of paper or, as a lot of publishers did, on a picture postcard which sold for a penny, could do so without fear of being prosecuted. My stablemate, Bob, who frequented the pub singing-rooms, had a very retentive memory for a tune and would bring it back the following morning and would either sing it or hum it, and so long as we got the tune we could soon get the words.

I remember him coming in one Sunday morning humming a tune: "By gum, lad, I heard a smashing song last night at pub. It goes like this: 'Delia, oh Delia.' I must get to know the words." It was many years before I found out that the song was "Velia" from the "Merry Widow" opera, but then neither of us knew the difference between operas and a musical revue. But we were both lovers of music and the fields often resounded with "Where the bees sucks there suck I," or "Hark hark the lark," or, by the time we got to the other end of the field, it would be "Keep the home fires burning."

There was another change coming over the farming world also, but no one noticed it. Many young fellows of military age or approaching it from well-to-do families were suddenly finding out that they, or their parents, had a great desire to be farmers, and the best way was to get a farmer friend or any farmer willing to take them on a work for meat basis. Many farmers jumped at the chance of free or nearly free labour. I will give credit where it is due; most of these that I met or heard of tried to earn their keep, but some of them brought a new look on to an old-fashioned outlook.

Also, the military were letting a lot of soldiers who were class B or C and were kicking their heels in camp doing nothing and learning nothing, come and work on farms. Sammy got three of them and one trainee from a wealthy Bradford family, a tall lad who hadn't a clue about farming but by jove he tried hard and in time he was like an old hand and Sammy was paying him. Nothing was a trouble to him, but at the end of the war, he went back to his father's business, and a good farmer was lost. But he and the soldiers opened a new world to the farming community with their outlook to farming and the conditions on some of the farms.

I remember one of them. He was the first man I ever saw wearing pyjamas. It tickled us all, and he was the recipient of a lot of ribald remarks when he put them on. But he called us a lot of "bloody heathen" and said we didn't know what comfort was, but I staggered him the next morning when he asked me where the toilet was. I pointed to the foldyard and told him there , or if he was working in the fields over the hedge. He raved, but I told him farms just didn't have such effeminate things and I never did find one or hear of one for the farm lads. He was full of scorn for the whole of the farming industry and the swede nawers in particular. He had been to public school but had chosen to join the army as a private. In time he found that he had to join the rest of us in our ablutions. As he remarked: "I can't hang out until I get my discharge, much as I hate it."

Most of the men mixed with the villagers wherever they were billeted and many a friendship was formed. But the biggest change was the different way of life that both the city and countryman found. Two of the soldiers that we got on our place had worked on farms in the south of England, so on the whole Sammy was not doing so badly for labour. We were also getting plenty of casual labour from Driffield from the older men who chose to work on the farms rather than some of the new jobs that were coming up in the town. But that source was to dry up before long when much better paid jobs were to be had building the new aerodromes that were springing up in the district.

I remember one such chap, old Nobby. He was a short stocky chap who chewed twist tobacco and was as stubborn as a mule on occasions. He was married to a Cockney who was as tall as he was short and with a temper to match, but except for an odd scrap when all the household goods seemed to get smashed, they lived together quite well. There were no children. It was said that his wife travelled up with one of the travelling circuses that called at Driffield on its travels and she decided to stay with Nobby, be what it may.

They were married, but as an instance of their married bliss, the foreman asked old Bob to call at Nobby's house one evening with a message about the next morning's work. So Bob duly knocked on the back door that evening and Daisy, that was his wife's name, answered the door. "Now then, what do you want?" she asked. "Is your boss in?" replied Bob. "Boss!" she snarled, "My boss in this bloody house, not likely, there's that twist-chewing old devil over there, will he do for you?" By that Nobby rushed from the fireside and grabbed her and within seconds there was a full scale battle going on. As Bob put it: "I didn't bother about the message, I just turned round and went home and thanked God that I was going on my own."

One morning Nobby came to work looking a bit worse for wear. Naturally there was a lot of ribbing, but after a while Nobby said: "Yes, we had a bit of a do last night. She was awkward as hell. I called at the Rose & Crown on me way home and I got talking and when I got in at ten o'clock, she'd chucked me dinner at back of fire and she started playing up. But I put her in her spot, properly." "It looks like it," remarked Jim quietly.

However, dinnertime arrived and the labourers with packed lunches sat down in the barn to have it, and as usual they were all wrapped in a white cloth and then a red handkerchief. Suddenly there was a shout from Nobby. "Look what she's bloody well done, she's wrapped it in newspaper, I'll be damned." It was almost a crime amongst country folk to wrap any food in newspaper. Then within seconds there was another shout: "And look what she's packed me, half a loaf of dry bread. Just wait until I get home tonight. I'll knock her blasted head off."

Next morning everyone was agog to know what had transpired and how Nobby got on, but there was no Nobby, so we all wondered who had won the night before. However, the next morning up stumped Nobby, tobacco juice running as usual, and after much questioning and ribbing it transpired that Daisy had refused to get up at 5 a.m. to get his breakfast ready, so after an argument he decided no breakfast, no work. But he couldn't do with two days off, so here he was still convinced he had won the day, but when he opened his dinner pack, he found who was the winner — she had packed four thick slices of bread burnt black and put two thick slices of raw turnip between them. He left us shortly afterwards to go to work on the new aerodrome that was being built near Driffield.

Time went on and we were very comfortable in the big house as regards food. There was a fantastic cook who could bake pies with a good crust and put plenty underneath it. Then out of the blue, we got a new hind; he came from Lincolnshire and had been working away from farming for some time, but the call of age was catching up with him so he returned to farming and the next week after he had arrived and got settled in, we went back to feeding in the hind's house again. We were loth to go, but that first breakfast, oh dear, boiled bacon and bread, no pie — to a Woldsman the lowest meal possible, having been brought up on beef three times a day and as much fruit pie as one wanted. There was immediate reaction, and the hind promised to have beef and pies the following morning.

He was big and blustering, and his wife was just the opposite, pale and wan, and with two sons who were about nine and ten, and he pushed her around. But could she cook? That was the big question us lads asked. Could she heck. She could make a pound of lard go beyond the bounds of possibility and a pound of jam she could spread across a fifty acre field — as we used to say, this pie has been twinked. Her rhubarb pies were shockers, with the sticks cut into lumps and put straight into the pie without any precooking, and the pie crusts were as tough as leather.

After one or two broken knives through trying to cut them we composed a little ditty:

> Her pies were made of sharps,
> Her bread was made of bran
> And it rattled in our bellies
> Like an old tin can.

Sharps, of course, was barley meal used for feeding pigs and some of the other stock. It was sometimes used by some country women in Wintertime to help out with the flour if bad weather prevented them from getting their supplies. But it had to have its lard well rubbed in and was purely a makeshift. However, the days rolled by and her cooking got no better. The pies were still tough and the beef greasy and tough, and the grumbles reached Sammy who immediately acted.

"Get the wife of one of the labourers to do the baking and don't mess about," he said. That altered the pie crusts, but not the filling. The hind's wife still controlled that, but they were eatable.

The foreman himself had not been used to our type of land and was a bit lost with the working of it until Sammy told him to use old Jim, one of the labourers, until he found his way round. But he couldn't find his way round old Charlie, the blacksmith. Charlie had lost a foot steel rule whilst measuring up a set of harrows in the yard and a fortnight later had seen the foreman with one exactly the same. When Charlie challenged him he declared that it was his own and refused to let him handle it to prove its ownership by Charlie's own mark on it. Sammy finally bought him a new one, but it rankled him that anyone could be so dishonest and deceitful.

Charlie was one of the fast disappearing band of local preachers who travelled from village to village every Sunday under their own steam. Some of them would walk to a village ten miles away, and take morning and evening service. Some of them had bicycles and would go even further. It had to be very bad weather to stop them, and of course there were some who were more popular than others and would fill the chapel for both services.

There were some villages that were more popular than others, too, because, as old Charlie put it: "Some tables are a lot heavier than others and you say grace with a lot more feeling at them spots." It was usual for someone in the village to invite the preacher to have his meals with them and , as he said: "I prefer not to see Missus at morning service." It meant that there would be a good hot Sunday dinner with roast beef and Yorkshire pudding. But if she was at chapel it meant that either dinner would be two hours late or it would be sandwiches and a cup of tea, and if you are leaving home just after six you were blooming hungry by twelve.

Without exception, they were a body of men who lived up to their principles of being Godly, righteous and sober-living people in their work and I was going to say play, but, as Charlie put it: "I never has time to play." Their spare time was taken up with the garden during the week. All tools were put away on Saturday evening. No work was done on Sunday, for to most country people Sunday was a day of rest. Sunday suits came out, clean shirts were put on which could be worn all the next week, and you would see men in twos and threes walking down the local lanes checking the work done on other farms with their own. Let there be one waver in the rows of corn or turnips, and there would be a full inquest on why and how the driver of the drill got such a dogleg in the row. Broadside fields drilled from the roadside as against drilling the same way as the road were always meticulously exact in distance from each other and as the seed sprouted, one had to be able to see every row from one side of the field to the other.

However, we are getting away from Charlie. One does hear it said: "The smith a mighty man is he," but that was not Charlie. He was small and dark, his hair always seemed to want cutting and his moustache usually covered his lips, but he was passionate in his speech and actions and one could at any time imagine him saying: "Won't one of you come and be saved!" On the farm where swear words were quite often used and tempers often frayed, Charlie never wavered. If a horse

45

leant on him when he was shoeing it, as many of the older horses did, either from pure boredom or cussedness, he would shout: "Wake up there!" and let the leg go with a thump.

But the older labourers used to say that he did lose his cool one day. On wet days or when a horse wanted shoeing, some of the lads would gather in the blacksmith's shop if there was not much doing in the work line. Well, this day, Charlie was heating and beating a piece of metal and kept putting it in the cooling tank and then heating it again. But one of the lads turned it round whilst Charlie's back was turned. Poor old Charlie got hold of the hot end. He shouted out and threw it straight at the one who had done it saying: "You rotten sod, you blasted heathen." Fortunately the metal missed the lad but went through the window. Charlie looked at his burnt hand and then, full of remorse for his explosion, closed his eyes and said: "Please God forgive me, but he was a rotten sod and one of us should have struck him dead." Sammy was so vexed about the rotten trick, he paid the lad off immediately.

In the days before the war started, Charlie had a donkey which Sammy let him keep in the small paddock with his hackney entires, and Charlie used the donkey to pull his little donkey-cart on Sundays during bad weather. I can remember him travelling in it about 1912 to 1914 and the ditty the lads used to chant as he passed:

"Hold the fort for I am coming in my donkey and cart.
The wheels are rotten and the shafts are broken,
But me donkey it won't start."

A craftsman at his trade, a popular man in his hobby, he stayed with us another few months, then the man service board caught up with him and he had to go to another town engineering. No one seemed to hear anything about him after that. He didn't want to go.

CHAPTER TEN

Spring came, bringing lighter nights and mornings and a little warmer weather, but it also meant longer hours of work. However, the wind of change was coming. The farm workers' union was getting stronger and their agitation for a shorter Saturday was bearing fruit. They had already got the Saturday knocking-off time moved from 6 p.m. to 5 p.m., which caused many farmers great distress and moans about their men working five short days and a little bit, and now it was rumoured that we were going to finish at one o'clock.

At last it arrived, the 1 p.m. finish, and before long it was 12 noon for everybody except the horseman and the beastman and the shepherd. We still had to feed the horses before breakfast and after tea, so it made very little difference to us. But for the weekly labourers it was a godsend. Previously nobody was paid on a farm until after finishing time on a Saturday, therefore the shopping was done late on Saturday night.

All shops remained open in Driffield until 10 p.m. and as a sign of how much money there was during the week, early closing day was Friday, years later to be changed to Wednesday. Market Day was always

Thursday when the town was packed by farmers and their wives, and the pub stables and yards would be filled with the trap horses and traps. The wife of the labourer would set off after breakfast from some of the Wolds farms pushing her pram with the two youngest in it the three to four miles into town to do her shopping and then push it back laden with her goods. Many used to push a pram even if they had no children or if they were at school. As more than one said: "I pushes pram at four miles an hour, but I only does three on my own." There were some champion walkers in those days — or pushers, whichever you care to call them.

But, as I was saying, Spring was here. The horses were going full tilt all the time as we tried to get the Spring corn in and the land ready for the turnip seed. The warmer weather made the horses sweat, and extra care had to be taken with the brushing and cleaning at night and checking for sore shoulders. Even so, a badly fittinged collar or one with uneven packing could make a sore place on a horse's shoulder during a morning's work.

Of course, a morning's work was from 6 a.m. to 12 noon, so on checking at dinnertime, one could find a sore patch three inches long and two wide. A horse, however big and strong, cannot stand pain or even discomfort. What other animals can get over easily can make a horse just lie down and not get up again. So a sore shoulder was a serious thing, and only time and care for a few days would cure it.

At that time of the year horses were indispensible, and when Charlie, our biggest and best horse, a really fine chestnut, got one, it was disaster. But our clever dick foreman said he had a cure for sore shoulder, a thing the best vets in the country had been looking for ever since horses were tamed and had failed to find. So we listened and looked when he brought this bottle of wonder-drops into the stable and went into Charlie's stall and poured some of it on the sore spot.

One could hear and see the flesh sizzle. Charlie screamed a blood-curdling scream. If one has heard the scream of a rabbit or hare at the point of being bitten by a dog after a chase and could multiply it tenfold, that was Charlie's scream. He threw himself back out of the stall, breaking his halter, and with eyes staring and mouth wide open he dashed into the foldyard. He was screaming and whinnying and kept galloping round and round until he dropped exhausted.

Poor old Charlie was completely demented because as soon as he could get overend again he stated stumbling round the foldyard, and if anyone went near him he rushed with mouth and jaws wide open. Finally we got him into one of the loose boxes in the yard and there he remained, fed over the side wall until after a few weeks he allowed old Bob to go near him. He never got better; he was always half mad, but Bob started to get a collar on him and he would work alongside Bob's mare Jenny.

The end came at harvest. One of the lads had him pulling the horse rake, but something upset him and he galloped across the field and tried to get through the gateway still yoked to the rake, hit the gatepost and dropped dead. Thus ended the life of a magnificent horse through a man's ignorance, a gentle creature that would take a piece of sugar from a baby.

Whatever failings Sammy might have had with his workers, his great pride was in his horses, hackneys or Shires, and as soon as he got to know about Charlie he sacked the foreman, told him to get off the farm and not come back. He said he would see that all he possessed in the farm was loaded up and sent to wherever he wanted it, and thus ended a worthless type of foreman and a woman who couldn't bake for "toffee." So it was back to Sammy's table, super cooking, with smashing pies which more than offset smoked tea and burnt milk.

We were very comfortable for a couple of weeks and then it arrived. If ever a tiger descended on a community it could not cause more upset than our new foreman. Sammy told us one mealtime that we would be going back into the hind's house for Monday morning. On Monday morning at twenty to six, we went in for breakfast, had good beef, well-cooked, good pies with plenty of "inside" to them, and then after breakfast the foreman descended into the stables.

"Look here, you mob," he said, "Your bedroom door through the wool chamber will be nailed up tonight and from here on you will come through the back kitchen, take your boots off and go up the back stairs to bed. Another thing, those damn smelly pots are coming out. I am not having my wife emptying those things. If you can't manage from 10 at night to five in the morning, you can come downstairs or bust!"

Cor! He stunned us, but the bedroom was getting like a pigsty. Wag said something. He had been properly spoilt by the last foreman and he was still much of a pig to me, but the new man shut him up quickly. "Thou hold thy gab," he said, "Thou has been as much at fault as the others and I am going through this spot like castor oil." (It was no wonder that we christened him Tiger from his very first day.) "And from tonight, groom's old saddle-room will be cleaned out and it will be for your use to sit in after you've finished with the horses." Previously we had sat in the stables or gone to bed. "And keep thy place clean," he added. The job, of course, came down the line to me as did making the fire each night. But he was a good foreman who knew his work and turned an undisciplined lot of men into a good-working and contented lot.

The horses were turned out into the pasture each night so we had free nights and weekends. But the pasture had a right of way through it so we couldn't lock the field gate across the road and you could bet that Tom, the shifty old rascal, would find a way once a week to get out of the field. We could turn him into the pasture and sometimes he would make straight to the gate and fiddle with the sneck with his nose. He could use his upper lip much as an elephant uses the tip of its trunk, to wriggle and wriggle, and if the sneck was at all loose he would lift it up and then quickly pull at the gate with his neck and as the gate opened he could go out.

Rarely did two get out because it would swing back behind Tom. But one was enough to have to chase after, more so if there were no signs as to which way the beggar had gone. But once or twice we had to fetch him from Driffield and had to pay for him to be released from the cattle pound that was then at the north end of the town. Finally, blacksmith Charlie made a special kind of sneck and a stile was made near the gate so that there was no need to open it quite so often, so we baffled old Tom and stopped his gallivanting.

That same Summer Sammy had three of his best hackney stallions struck by lightning as they were sheltering under a tree in the front paddock. He had a groom, a proper old reprobate if ever there was one. He never seemed to be without a cigarette in his mouth; it was always a Woodbine at five for a penny. Why worry if you coughed your inside up every morning and every penny you had to spare was spent at the Rose & Crown in Driffield.

He completely ignored the farm staff except to grumble that the clover stack was always built at the furthest point from his stables and the wheat straw for his bedding was always damp — a queer race were grooms. But he was supposed to be the best man in the district for getting a hackney up to London show standards. I remember looking at all his rosettes won at various shows.

He also looked after the farm horses from being foals to their being broken in to working gears, through castration and tail shortening or "strunting," as it was called, which was undoubtedly the most barbaric practise on a farm. They were usually done whilst they were foals, but quite often one of them got left or no one bothered until the poor creature was probably two years old then the operation became a major one.

The young horse would have the twitch put on its nose — a horrible practise that should be banned completely. The object of the twitch was to tighten it by twisting a stick about thirty inches long with a string loop on the end, round the soft part of the horse's nose until the pain caused by the twisting took precedence over anything else that was being done to the animal. The groom would have the cutting iron ready and the strunting cup heating in a fire and the Stockholm bar. One man would be using the twitch and one holding the tail. Crunch would go the iron, followed quickly by the hot cup over the tail to stop the bleeding, off with the cup, a handful of the tar would be rubbed on the tail end, amid screams from the poor victim, and as the twitch was released a shudder would go through the horse. There would be no comments from the men unless it was "poor sod," and it would be left in the loose box to gather itself together again.

I suppose anything else would hate human beings for ever after that, but even so, it was no worse than the castration operation on a stallion that had probably been serving mares for a season and had been proved to be of no use as a sire. Thus he would be of no value as a stallion and would have to be castrated and broken in to work alongside the other horses.

The same procedure was followed — a twitch on the nose, hobbles on all four feet joined by pullies to a rope which when pulled by two or three men drew all the legs together until all the hooves touched. Then the horse was given a push and over he went on his side then rolled onto his back. After two quick cuts the two clams, which were usually of elderberry wood, were put on the cords and tightened up, and with another two sharp cuts it was all over. He could be released and what was once a proud specimen of arrogance was now just another carthorse. That was a time when one did get remarks of sympathy from the men. But tail cutting and castration was usually carried out whilst the animals were young and was a job that most country labourers could do, but when the animal was adult they preferred the vet to come and operate.

The usual end to an entire that had been castrated was to let him rest for a couple of weeks, then he would be brought into the stable with the other horses. A collar would be put over his head to fit his shoulders — the final indignity — and a pair of traces over his back. Off he would go with the oldest and slowest horse, to be yoked to some implement and then, instead of being broken in to all gears, he would be worked in to all gears. Putting him with an old and slow horse meant that he would be tied on a short halter rope to the older one no matter how he tried to rush and push. Through the method of yoking and swingle and kipple tree gearing to the implement, he would either be pulling it on his own, which in time tired him out, or if he tried to go too fast and pushed the older horse, he could get a sharp bite on the nose.

He would find out that he had dropped very low in the peck order, so that after a week or two of that sort of punishment he would learn the first lesson about work — the more you do, the more you may! But whatever treatment they got, they were always temperamental and not to be relied on. We had one at a farm I worked on that had been cut for a year or two, got the scent of one of the mares in season, went rampant, turned the set of harrows he was pulling over and got so entwined with his traces and the swingle trees that he threw himself onto the sharp harrow points, injuring himself so severely that he had to be put down.

CHAPTER ELEVEN

It was harvest time and the Irishmen were back again for the extra money they could earn in the English harvest fields. They were without exception all hard workers, and nearly everything was done by piecework. Most of them came to the same farms year after year, and as one got too old to come or unable to, it would be young Jim or Mick who would take his place. At the end of each harvest they would make arrangements for the next one and never was a farmer let down by them or by the quality of their work. They made good money but they earned it.

Most of them came for the hay-time in the West Riding and came on to corn country for harvest. Some would then move on to the potato districts for a few weeks before going home again, and I still remember one of the plaintive songs they taught me:

"Far, far away on the banks of the Nile,
Thousands of miles from his own green isle
Stood a brave Irish soldier lad, a gallant dragoon
Who reads his Mother's letter by the light of the moon.
Is it true, too true, more trouble in my native land.
He stole from his camp the sweet note to read
The news that it brought made his down heart bleed
For while Pat was fighting at the head of his band
His Mother had been convicted and lost all her land.
Is it true, too true, more trouble in my native land."

But for us harvest time meant work from dawn to dark. Hours were not counted, nor was the clock. The labourers went out with the scythe at 6 a.m. to "open out" a field, which meant scything a full sweep of the scythe all the way round the field ready for the binders to be pulled into the field and then getting them off their travelling wheels and the yoking pole put in its proper place for the horses.

Most of the binders in the Wolds district had a six foot cut at the time (the seven foot came a year or two later), so that meant four horses to pull each one, two in front of two. The driver rode the nearside back one and always travelled anti-clockwise, so he rode the horse just in front and to the right of the cutting blades. It was hard luck for the driver if the horse he was riding stumbled, or, like one on the farm next to us, trod in a rabbit hole and threw its driver in front of the blades.

Fortunately the man riding the reaper had quick reactions and pulled the height cutting lever full towards him lifting the blades to their highest point off the ground, thus allowing the driver's body to pass underneath the canvas which collected the cut corn and carried it into the machine to be bundled and tied and thrown out on to the ground. The man riding the reaper also shouted "Whoa" to the horses and they stopped quickly, but George the driver was underneath the machine, badly mangled. He was rushed to hospital as quickly as a horse-drawn rully could take him. He came out of hospital about a year later, minus one eye and with a permanent limp and an arm that never worked properly again. He got back to work as a roadman in his native village. The Great War was still on and it was work that he could do.

The method of cutting the standing corn has changed very little since the first reaper was made, the old-fashioned Bamlet drawn by two horses. It cut the corn and left it behind in a neat swathe ready for the harvesters to tie up into sheaves. The cutting blades were V-shaped and about four inches wide. They were riveted in close succession onto a flat rod which was pulled and pushed from a drive and gears by a wheel which turned as the horses pulled the machine. The blades ran on a runner which had metal points on it protecting the blades and parting the corn into the way of the blade.

The huge modern combines still use the original method, but the length of the cutters has gone up from three or four feet to eighteen and twenty feet, and one combine can now harvest the grain from a twenty-acre field in one day. With the balers rolling those huge bales of straw weighing upwards of fifteen hundredweight following up, a field of waving corn at eight a.m. can be a field of stubble at eight p.m.

A wet harvest is bad enough even with the modern methods of gathering it in, but try to imagine the frustration of wet day after wet day. What was worse still was a week's fine weather at the beginning of the harvest month so as to get a good proportion of the corn cut, by the old method of the stookers following up the binders, every stook with its equal number of sheaves, each two propping each other up, six or eight at each side, pointing north and south to get maximum sun on each side. When the men finished stooking a field it really did look a picture, and then down would come the rain.

The stooks would get wet through, then there would be a fine day and the order would come: "Get those stooks turned!" and everyone except the boss would go to old Mossy Brown or Nab End field (every field on a farm has its name) to turn the sheaves round and re-stook them. Simple? Yes, try it when the sheaves are wet and you have to handle them under each arm and let them slide down and drop in their new positions with the outsides now inside.

Leading clover at S. R. Tennant's Great Kendale Farm, near Driffield, in 1916. Some of the staff, with H. Reffold sat on the ground at the right of the photograph.

Often a dozen stooks had been moved. We lightweights would be wet through from the armpits down. The older, stronger men could handle them by picking them up by the heads and holding them away from their clothing, but they could still be wet from the knees down, and so it would go on until the sun got out and some of the stooks would be dry enough for loading to the stackyard.

We also would have nearly dried out, but not to worry, we had to get back to the stables, get the horses yoked to the wagons and get them back into the field. If the sun kept shining we would dry out. In spite of the discomfort and being completely wet through, none of seemed to have any secondary effects. When you are young and getting plenty of good food you can take an awful lot of punishment and still thrive.

If the sun was still shining after dinner, all horses were yoked to wagons, two to each one. The first pair would set off at the trot. "Hurry up, get a small load and get back. Let's get the stack moving upwards. We've got five wagons going. You take that stack, Wag, and I'll carry on with the one we started last week." That's the foreman shouting about. "Don't stand there lad, poking thy nose. Get yoked up and get down to the field. Thou hasn't got a saddle — get a sack or else ride the blamed horse bareback. What! Thou'll get a sore backside. Clear off or my boot will give you a proper sore backside."

With the sun shining and a good breeze the corn was drying. The Boss's temper was a bit short: "Careful Harry lad, get on that horse and get down to the field. Never mind your bottom, you have had it sore before!" Yes, but I shall never forget it. Daisy, a big fat Shire mare with a pedigree a mile long and a temper to match, and as a jibber she had no equal. She had come into service after the entires had finished travelling, so Sammy decided she should be taken to the stud farm eight miles away. So at six o'clock off we went, me riding bareback.

By the time we reached Driffield I was beginning to feel sore and Daisy was sweating and my cord trousers were wet. By the time we were halfway I was walking and leading Daisy. When we got there and brought the entire out she was having none of it, and then I got into trouble with the groom. I hadn't brought his shilling, which was his fee for all mares served or tried which was paid separate from the pound service fee.

Even now when I pass that lane end leading to the farm I think about that. Just over eight miles walk back, a sore bottom, trousers stiff with horse sweat and chafing the top of my legs with every step, and it was a hot June day. And when I got back to the farm, no sympathy, no one to say we must do something about that lad's bottom. No, it was "Get her yoked into the horse rake and get started raking that clover field." I may say that underpants were never worn by the younger lads in those days.

But we are now harvesting down in the corn field. The first wagon was loaded and coming out. There was an elegance about a wagon load of corn sheaves, with each sheaf laid perfectly straight in its proper place. First the wagon bottom was filled head to tail full length, then twice all round the sides, heads inward, then we would fill the middle again, then one course at the front, heads inwards and fastened by another row, reversed and reaching to the band round the last straw, then the rear end. Then we did the same reducing the width of the load by one sheaf each row, finishing with a two and then one at each end and a sloping middle, thus making it easier for the man forking the sheaves to the loader.

It was a skilful job to prepare a full load of sheaves that would stand the rocking and jerking across the bumpy fields. Many were the mishaps of loads slipping or being fastened with ropes and pulled tight enough for it to reach the stackyard. Even then, the inexperienced loader could have one shoot and leave half his load in a heap behind him.

Even in these days how many of us have followed or passed one of those huge lorry loads of baled straw travelling from our corn-growing areas to the dairy farming country and admired the precision of the load and its size and thought what a skilful bit of work had been done by the loader making sure that every single bale was in its correct place and that every bale was fastened by another one the oppose way. Half a dozen misplaced bales in a load could mean a slide after a sudden stop or on a bumpy road. Loading straw or sheaves is a skilful job and requires intense concentration if a load of from four to five hundred bales has to kept absolutely plumb and square for a long journey.

But back to our horse and wagons and the stack which by now is starting to show shape and size. The size usually meant that when completed it would be a full day's threshing, so if it was a hired threshing machine, the stack had to take all the day and not go into the next one otherwise the machine would either go to the next farm and leave a part stack or if the owner was not so busy he would charge for a full day extra.

The stacker had to measure the base of his stack very carefully and make it the right height. At eight p.m. it would be getting dusk and we were tired out. The foreman shouts: "Hey lad, hurry up, thou just has time for another load. What's thou muttering about? I'll be off this stack to thou if thou doesn't hurry up and get off and bring the forkers back with thee; they will be ready for night!"

So off we go and get a small load. The three men who have been forking the sheaves are riding on the part load. They drive back to the stackyard, unyoke the horses, and take them straight to the stables. The last man in takes the collars off the horses and gives them a feed. By this time Wag shouts: "Supper." We haven't had a bite since louances at 4 o'clock, or a drink either. We gobble our supper of cold beef, bread and lumps of pie washed down by gulps of weak tea, then it's back to the stable, feed and brush the horses for another hour, then turn them out into the horse pasture for the night.

It's now ten o'clock. We fetched them up at 4.30 a.m. and will do the same tomorrow morning. Thus ends a seventeen-and-a-half hour day, and if it keeps fine all the week it will be the same each day except Saturday, which is a short day, finishing at 6 p.m. Sunday is a day of rest. The horses just could not stand working seven days a week. As for the men, that's what we were hired to do. As youngest lad I got £6-10 shillings. Wag as top paid man got £22 for the year. No wonder that when a union man appeared on the scene his talk fell on fertile ground.

CHAPTER TWELVE

"All is safely gathered in
E'er the Winter storms begin."

But before that comes along the stacks have to be made waterproof, and that was where Jim, the oldest labourer, came into his own. I used to think that he was one of the ancients, but I found out that as one gets older, the old ones don't alter, because I met Jim fifteen years later. He had left Sammy and was working for the Council and talking about retiring in a year or two's time, but that is by the way.

"Hey lad," said the foreman one morning, "go and help Jim with the thatching. He wants somebody with him, and thou is the best we can offer." Compliments, like sympathy, were not overworked on a farm. I didn't mind going to Jim. I liked him and his wife was a kindly type who used to fuss us lads up a bit. They had no children and they were Church as against Charlie the blacksmith and his wife, who were Chapel. Each used to sniff at the other and they lived in adjoining cottages on the farm. Jim liked a glass of beer and Charlie called it hell's poison.

However, back to our stacks. They had to be preared for thatching. All the loose straw was taken off the top and the ends of the sheaves flattened and any slack places were filled in with straw laid flat and wetted to make it solid. The sides were trimmed with a cutter usually made out of a broken scythe fastened on the end of a shaft of wood about four feet long. When sharp it was amazing how easily one could cut awkward lumps on the side of the stack where a few carelessly laid sheaves had started to slide and by the time Jim had finished cutting and trimming, the stack was plumb and ready for thatching.

"Fetch some of that wheat straw from that stack over there!" said Jim. "It's good thatching stuff; we put it through the machine when we were threshing it specially for this job, and it's good long straw and not smashed up. Bring a good pile of it and put it just down there then I'll show thee what to do with it." Right, so off I went with a pitchfork and soon had a pile big enough for him.

"Look," said Jim. "This is what you do. Stand with thy feet together and pull the straw in handfuls from the heap and lay it straight on thy boots until it reaches thy knees, then get as much of it as thou can hold in one hand, get hold of each end and pull it apart. Do it quickly giving it a shake outwards which sends all the small straw flying, then bring it together again and put it in a real tidy heap behind thou ready for wetting and putting on the top."

I soon got the hang of the job and the pile of straight straw began to grow. "That's enough for now," said Jim. "I've got my bands and sticks out of the shed so we'll start at this side. Let's put the ladder up. That's it, leaning full length on the roof of the stack, from the top to the eaves." He then tied a piece of string to one of the spells. "What's that for?" I enquired. "Ah," replied Jim, "that's the depth of the eaves. The first row of thatch is level with that band and thus the first layer all the way round. It makes a better finish. Come on then, let's have some water! Fetch a can full from the pond and we'll damp the straw and get on with the job."

Once the straw had been wetted, up the ladder went Jim, a small bundle of straw with him which he proceeded to get in handfuls and double over and push into the stack leaving about nine inches sticking out. He did this for a distance of eighteen inches. He then shouted for his thatching twines, lengths of binder twine wrapped round thin pieces of wood with a point on, which he stuck into the stack after fastening one end of the string to a thatching peg thrust into the top as near level as possible. As Jim said, we don't want any water running down the peg. If you put a couple of hundred pegs in your thatching pointing down, that meant a couple of hundred wet spots on threshing day.

He then came down the ladder and put his leather kneecaps on. Your knees got a bit sore without any protection when you'd been at it a few days. "Come on lad," he said, "let's get some straw on. If we don't make a bit of a show Sammy will sack both of us." So he gathered an armful of the straw and went up the ladder and started to put it in layers about three inches deep covering one third of each layer by the next one, eighteen inches wide, right to the top, with me carrying fresh straw as he called for it up the ladder.

Fresh pegs were then pushed in alongside the ladder and the bands were fastened to them to keep the newly laid straw firm and tight after he had battened it down with a wooden batten and raked all the straw completely straight with a small hand rake. It took one day for a small stack and two for a large one, and it wasn't long before all the stacks were covered. Real smart they looked too after Jim had trimmed the eaves with his shears. I quite well remember him saying: "Yes lad, thou learn to thatch. They will always want thatchers on farms." How wrong he was, and how soon.

Once harvest was over we began muck-spreading from the foldyards onto the fields that were to be drilled with wheat during October. Some of the manure had been taken from one of the yards during the Summer and stacked in one of the fields and I remember loading my cart with the help of Bob and Nobby, when I dug into a pile of bones and putrid flesh. I didn't know at that time that when a sheep died the usual way was for the shepherd to take the skin and fleece off the animal and then bury the remains in the manure hill where it soon seemed to disappear.

But when I found those bones excitement mounted and I was sure that there had been a murder and the body put there out of sight. I said he seemed to have been a small person, and Nobby said: "Yes, I've often wondered what become of that cheeky youth last year and I'll tell thou now Joe lad that some of those keen foremen soon bash anybody that's lazy and cheeky to them on top of their napper and bury them in muck hill."

"But," I said, "these bones are different jaw bones to ours." "That's right," said Bob, "I allus thought he was a queer youth." "Yes, but didn't his folks miss him?" I asked. "Yes, I believe they did," replied Bob, "but we told them he had run away so they did not bother any more." Naive? Yes, but you learn very quickly on a farm.

The next few weeks we were busy with drilling the wheat. We used four two-horse ploughs and then the drill, which took the four rows at a time and pressed the soil between each furrow with the specially shaped wheels and allowed the corn to drop from the seed container direct into the groove. It would then be harrowed in by a following team.

On November 23rd came Martinmas Day, that day long awaited by all the hired men when all those who were, in their own words, sick and tired of the blooming spot and were just waiting to kick the last bit off muck off their boots and get away and those who were content to stay on the place for another year — provided the "Gaffer" asked them to — were to be paid off and could look forward to a week's holiday (without pay) and not have to get up in the dark to feed the horses or cattle or whatever.

The only holiday recognised by farmers was the week from the 23rd November to the 1st December, when all those who had been hired had to be back on the farm. The only other holiday was Christmas Day, which was the men's own in between feeding stock. The labourers housed on the farm were not even considered with regard to holidays. They just didn't get them and if any of them worked amongst stock, such as in the sheepfold in Winter, every day was just another day and they would most likely be paid two shillings a week extra. Oh, the thousands of extra hours worked by the tied cottage labourers for an extra two shillings and in many cases for a pint of flat beer.

But here we were. It was the 23rd, pay day. We lined up at Sammy's back door in the middle of the afternoon, in order of seniority or peck order. First came the senior horsemen; after them the shepherd and beastman and their lads followed by the waggoners lad, then came my moment. The maid took me through to the lounge, and there was Sammy huddled over a most miserable fire and wearing his old black overcoat, mittens, and a shawl round his shoulders. He always had, or so it was said and I believed it, a teapot full of water at the fireside and as the fire or fire logs started to burn up damped the fire down. Extravagance was not one of his vices. He counted greed as a virtue.

"Now Harry, sit down on that chair," he started. "Your year is up and it's now pay day and I have just checked the book and I see you have had no subs during the year." I agreed. "And now are you stopping again with me for another year?" I replied: "No, I don't like Wag or his brother," and now I had a chance I was off. "Well, well," said Sammy, "I didn't like them either so I didn't ask them to stay so now what?" I still demurred.

"Well, now then my boy, how much money do you want?" "£6 ten shillings," I answered. "Oh no," said Sammy. "£6 was agreed last Martinmas and another ten shillings if you were a good lad." "Well, I have been a good lad." "Oh yes, but you haven't finished yet until I pay you and I say you will not be a good lad if you don't stop again, so there." Frustration! I was full of it, so I said: "Right, if you don't give me it I will stand in Driffield Market Place on hiring day and shout and tell everybody how mean you have been."

That sat him up. "Come, come laddie, I didn't mean it. I will give you your ten bob, so here you are, six one pound notes and look, a golden half sovereign for luck." I wish very often that I could have kept that gold coin, the first and last time I received a gold coin as wages, but it was one thirteenth of my wages for one year and there were bills to be paid in Driffield.

"Now that we have got that settled and you get on all right with the foreman and he has engaged another waggoner," continued Sammy, "I think you couldn't do better than stop with us for another year." So after a lots of hums and haws I agreed. "That's good," he said. "How much do you want for the year?" "£11," I replied. "Good heavens that's nearly as much as a man gets, and don't forget thou is still not very big." "That's nothing; there are lots of jobs I can do just as well as the bigger ones, and besides I am now fifteen."

"I know, I know," was the answer, "but there are a lot of jobs you cannot do, so don't talk like that. I'll tell you what I'll do. I like you, otherwise I wouldn't dream of it. I will give you ten pounds for the year and if you are a good lad for another year I'll give you another ten shillings," and he grinned at me. I said; "Right, ten pounds ten shillings and five bob fest!" "Oh dear no, I am not giving all that money and a five shilling fest, not likely. I will give you half-a-crown fest. I can't afford to throw money about like that. Right then, you'll take the half crown and be a good lad and be back on the farm a week today."

Clutching my £6 ten shillings in my pocket I set off for Driffield to stay with one of my aunts for the night. I really felt one of the world's wealthiest men, but the thought was tempered when I started to think about the bills I had to pay the following day. I also had to repay my father for the money he had subbed me during the year for my pocket money and small things I had had to buy.

However, after a night's rest off I went, first to Fred Hornby, the tailor, where one suit, handmade, cost 19/-, and with two heavy working shirts and one or two other oddments, bang went £2. I wanted two pairs of boots, one for working, one for Sundays, and they were 3/- per pair. I paid my aunt 10/- for the year for washing my shirt and one pair of socks weekly.

Fred Hornby measured me for another suit and some more working trousers. "Pay some of the money now lad and pay the rest next Martinmas." That was how all the country tailors worked in those days, on trust, and very rarely was that trust broken. It was the same with the boot makers; they would measure your feet and produce the most fantastic boots — light or heavy. As old Jabez Pickering told me when I asked him for some: "Thou is too young for these boots. Thy feet are still growing and they will be too small for thee before they are barely worn. You buys these boots of mine to last for years and if they wears I can put new tops on them or new soles and I puts a patch on them, anywhere, and they will cost you fifteen bob. I don't like making them for anybody over forty because they always die before they get them worn out, and they never seem to fit anybody else."

This was the true pride of a craftsman, and practically every village had one or two craftsmen and some of the larger places had their blacksmith and joiners. Some of them also had wheelwrights who were well-known outside their own parish for their skill in the making of carts and wagons, each one made exactly the same as the last one with the maker's own style of painting. They were always a talking point amongst the farm hands, who discussed the merits of Sissons of Beswick as against other makes, but the last years have proved that they rotted out quicker than they wore out.

A farmer could buy one new when he started farming and it would be handed down to his sons and grandsons, but when the light, all-metal trailer came on the scene the poor old wagon was left out in all weathers in a corner of the stackyard where it probably brooded over its former glory when it came into the yard with a huge load of sheaves of wheat on it, drawn by Wag's pair of dapple greys and the foreman saying; "That's the finest load of corn I have ever seen!"

But we are romancing just too much. Foremen never gave compliments. It was either: "We've been waiting for you half an hour," or "Don't be so damn long next load."

But there the old wagon rested in yard or field corner until some day someone with no sentiment whatever came along and cleared the corner up, and all that once solid oak, ash and elm was pulled onto a heap and burned. Whilst he was at it he probably threw away the old choppy cutter and the turnip cutter and an old scruffler and horse rake, and to make up a load for the scrap man chucked the last of their horse ploughs. He would be a few pounds better off, but posterity was worse off.

CHAPTER THIRTEEN

Martinmas week soon passed — a few days at home in Hull with Dad and my sister and two nights at the theatre. There were four live theatres in Hull at that time and what was on didn't matter so long as there was singing that I could listen to and remember, to be able to take back to my stable mate Bob. The fact that I could only manage to afford the "gods" did not matter.

I remember I dearly wanted a bicycle, but a new one was out of the question and as a decent secondhand one would cost me thirty shillings I was thwarted there. I had only ten bob left of my six pounds ten shillings and Dad said he was broke, so I had to do without for another two years. I had no fairy godmothers or relations either. If you hadn't it you didn't get it, as simple as that.

On December 1st it was back to Sammy's. There were fresh faces all round: a fresh Wag, a new third lad, Bob still in his stable in the corner, another Wag's lad, a fresh shepherd's lad, same beastman, old Bill and his lad Charlie. When we horsemen gathered together in the stable that night I found that I had been promoted to thirdy's lad and that I was not now the youngest lad.

Sammy had hired a youngster of thirteen. He was called Len and had left school the day he was twelve and had one year's farming experience and had been lucky enough to get on a good farm near to where his parents lived. His father was a farm labourer and he had been quite a favourite with the farmer's wife who, he told me, used to make sure that he was well wrapped up during the bad weather and gave him one of her daughter's mufflers. If he got wet through she made sure that his clothes got well dried.

I asked him why he didn't stop again for another year. He said that his younger brother was now twelve and had left school and he was taking his place. There were three girls older than him all in domestic service and six younger than him. The house they lived in was a farm tied cottage, two up and two down. The only water supply was the same as in so many country cottages, rain water from the roof running into a barrel after being filtered through an old sack fastened on the end of the down spout.

He had not been taught to either read or write at school, a not uncommon thing in the country of those days unless the youngster had a natural ability, and in that case the school master quite often took an extra interest in him. For the next year I wrote all his letters and read those he received for him. We got on really well together for that year, but after he left I never saw him again. Years later I went past where he had lived, but the cottage was derelict, so I drove on.

Wag was an older man than the last year's one; an experienced chap, his word was respected. He had worked on many of the large farms on the Wolds. He and Bob got on like old pals. They both had originated from the Wolds village of Weaverthorpe, but Bob had left school before the other one had started. They both had decided ideas on how to feed horses. The previous year Bob had had it all his own way. Our four horses (I call them our four even if I didn't feed them) were the fattest, the fittest and best-looking in the stables.

By now old Daisy, the mare that Sammy used to pull his trap to market, was getting too fat for the shafts and it would not be long before it would have to be wider shafts or a fresh horse. But his pride and joy, Beaulah, was to be sold. A buyer from Leeds had been to see him and a vet was coming to check him, and if he passed him Bob would be taking him to Driffield station for the last time and from then he would be a brewery horse pulling rully loads of beer around Leeds.

Before he went into the horse box Bob had him weighed in the station yard. He weighed just a ton. Not many horses reach a ton. It is not the amount of food or any particular blend of oats and chaff you give the horse that makes the difference. A little too much corn and your horse may stall and refuse food and has to be hungered back to eat. If they are working hard at the time, it could create problems, and no animal shows its condition quicker or more emphatically than a horse, be it mare or gelding. As for entires, as the grooms used to say: give them a couple of oats upside down in their crib and they would have bellyache after the shock.

Casual labour was now getting rather scarce. The war effort was in full swing and a big new aerodrome was being built at Driffield. The difference in wages and working hours made sure where it went. But we could still get soldiers for farm work, so we were not so badly off, and it was remarkable how quickly some of them settled down to farm work. Of course there was always the thought that it was better than the Somme, and it was a sure bet that if a soldier was returned to barracks as unsuitable he would soon be on a draft for overseas.

There were still one or two of the older Rangers about and old Drover Jack was one of them who had got too old for cattle droving. I had seen him knocking about the Driffield market for a year or two and he had stayed at Aunt Jane's lodging house many times, but time and his way of living was telling on him, and another Winter or two would find him a victim of exposure and pneumonia. But he was, to me, a wonderful talker when he told about his life as a drover.

He told us one day in our bothy that his father was a drover before the railways came on the scene when cattle were driven from Scotland down to London or from the boats at Liverpool to all parts of the country. His father had come down with some beasts from the north to the West Riding and there he met Jack's mother and married her.

She bore him four children before the droving itch caught up with him again and he went down south with his dog and a mate and she never saw him again. Life was more than rough for them. His mother had been the worker whilst his fatherr had done very little else but poaching or small droving jobs from the local farms to the nearest cattle markets. Four children under six was too much for her. She contracted consumption, her two youngest died and the other two went into an orphanage. Jack was sent out to work when he was twelve into the farm and his sister into domestic service at the same age. After that, they drifted apart and they had not seen each other since.

Every drover had one or two dogs, one of which was usually a lurcher. As Jack neatly put it, there was one to do the work and one to provide your dinner. It was interesting watching the drovers in the market after they had delivered their cattle to the pens and received their payment for the job. Most of them shot straight off to the pub until the selling got under way, then they would return to look for a return job.

As each lot was sold it would be noted who to and there would be a rush to the farmer for the droving and then the haggle would start. "How much will you do it for? I'll give the three shillings." "No maister, it's six miles to your spot, I'll do it for four." Most farmers would haggle just for sheer cussedness, but some did it for pure greediness. The drovers got to know them quickly and it was a last job if they took their beasts.

"It's a lot, Jack, is four shillings. Say three and sixpence and a supper when you get them on the farm." "All right then maister, but thou's a hard nut. If my dogs knew how much I'm getting they would not go with me. I'll tell you what maister, I haven't had a drink all day, I've only got a ha'penny in my pocket. Give me tuppence to make it a pint and the job is on."

By ten o'clock the cattle, sheep or bullocks would be in the paddock after a gentle drive from the market, the farmer knowing full well that if he had cut the price his beasts would have been driven fast and would have arrived dead beat and taken a week to get over it. Jack would get his supper and be told that he could stay the night in the barn and to mind where he put his pipe before he dozed off.

Next morning he would be back at the back door trying to beg a piece of pie and a mashing of tea from the maids. Then he would be on his way, his teacan on his belt, all his wordly possessions in his pocket, keeping a lookout for a hare. It would be a good hare that got away if his lurcher got a sight of it and the hare would be worth ninepence if he could get it to the butcher in the next village. Rabbits were only worth a few pence and he usually fed his dogs on them.

The drover fulfilled an important part in the working of the country life, but his end was in sight when the railways started carrying cattle. Many of us can still remember those wagons with their barred sides, and one can still see at some of the village stations a raised platform on a siding with railings round it where the animals were driven and then herded into the wagons. But the end came when those huge transport lorries came and the droving of livestock was forbidden in the streets of the cattle market towns.

The drovers lived a hard independent life and few of them made old bones, but as characters they stood out. I remember some of them well and their nicknames; few, if any, seemed to have a surname. Soldier

Bob's pal was known as Corporal, and there were Cottam Dick and Lofty Jack. He had his favourite droving run from Driffield over the Wolds towards Malton via Sledmere and Duggleby, then to pick up a run to Malton market and returning the following week. Droving could be difficult during hot weather. After they left Duggleby for Driffield there were few watering places until Driffield Beck was reached, so it was ether early morning or late evening travel in Summer to get the cool dew-drenched roadside grass.

The months passed by. I was now nearly sixteen, and as Sammy remarked to me, there was no fear of me being a jockey now. The good table that the hind kept made growth and strength come naturally, although my faith in his wife's cooking got a nasty shock when one evening I wandered into the kitchen to find her two sons throwing crusts at one another. "Hey," I said, "Don't you know there's a war on? Wasting bread!" "It isn't wasted," replied the older one, "Me Mam saves all crusts up each week and then she soaks them in water and makes your berad pudding with them." I went off bread puddings from then on and except when I was forced to, I have never had one since.

Winter went on, bringing cold miserable jobs, but I now had someone younger than me to share all the rotten jobs that the senior chaps could dodge. On a cold, wet or snowy day the foreman would announce: " We will have those thorns gathered up and burnt in that top field!" which meant one of us or both yoking a horse into a cart and going with one or two men to gather the hedge cuttings that the hedge slasher had chopped off.

We would get to the field, senior "peck" would then order lowest "peck" to get into the cart and load the thorns as they were forked up to him. We then stood in the cart shivering until some thorns had been gathered into heaps ready for them to be forked on to the cart. The first few forkfuls were all right, but as the load got higher each time the horse pulled on over the rough ground it became more difficult to keep overend, and when leading "peck" would command the horse to "gee up" without first giving the usual notice "hold hard" you were flung either backwards or forwards onto the bed of thorns. Cold, wet or frozen you had to say: "It's OK, thirdy," when he remarked "Sorry kid," and he was already sniggering at your discomfort with his mate.

Finally there were enough thorns on the cart. "Right lad, get down, hurry up, we haven't all day to stick here. Shut thine eyes and walk about a bit, thou will soon be down." At last on firm ground. "Right lad, take it over to yon bit of straw and we will warm the field up a bit." Tip the load up, lift the cart back, put the joggle stick back, watch them light the fire, go for a warm up, to be told: "We can manage the fire, thou take the rake and tidy up where we've finished."

You must not mutter or be heard muttering or a boot was soon helping you on your way "and to be a farmer's boy, and to be a farmer's boy." Never mind, another year or two and you would be a bit higher in the peck order, but you say to yourself: "Yes, but I won't be such a rotten so-and-so to the least lad," and the next morning except for a pair of tattered leggings and a hole in your trousers where the wind blows through you have forgotten all about it.

On the other hand it might have been Len who had been leading the thorns and had exactly the same treatment, and the foreman might have said to me: "It's over wet to plough. Take two horses and fetch some turnips up for the beastman Bill." As it was just starting to come light I would put the collar and cart saddle on Prince, who would be thinking: "It would be me on a morning like this." Then you put the traces on Tinker and the same thoughts were shared again.

Every farm had its one or two "turnip horses." They were usually old horses that were still useful for odd jobs but were getting past keeping up with the younger ones. It comes to everything that works, but in their case it finished up with a humane killer. I've heard more than one old labourer crippled with arthritis say: "Lucky blighters!"

However, we got our two horses yoked to the cart, our short fustian leggings and overcoat on, and a railway sack over our shoulders as a cape. Then off we would go down the muddy lane, and as we get away from the buildings we would meet the full blast of the wind. We walked alongside the cart to get a little shelter, and then turned into the turnip field and up to the shepherd's hut.

He and his shepherd lad would have got a fire going in his little hut, and we would take a few minutes to ask where to get the turnips from. Four rows at a time were pulled for the cattle, leaving a number of rows for pulling and cutting into fingers by the turnip cutter. The shepherd tells us to go to the bottom of the field and start another four rows and to mind that we left two rows for him.

It's not raining now, but by gum it's cold. We drive down the field and set the horses in the rows to be pulled. There is still a fair amount of top on the turnips. We grab one by the top, it comes up easy, then we pull one in each hand, knock them together to loosen the soil off, then throw them into the cart. The wet leaves soak our sleeves almost to the elbow; your wrists are still chapped and sore from the last lot of turnips we fetched.

We soon forget the cold and the cart fills up, turnip on turnip, until it's loaded at last. "Gee up Tinker, come on Prince." I jump on the front of the cart and then scramble on Prince's back. The mud and slurry at the field gate is a foot deep and my legs are wet enough already so I take the "easy" way and ride back to the farm, tip the load into the turnip house for the beastman, who tells me that he wants another load or two, so off we go again, miserable and wet, and there were no rubber wellingtons in those days. Still, we dried out and thought about Summer when we could go down to the fields with our jackets off.

Weeks passed and the warm weather came. Corn drills rattled and the foreman became more and more keen to get the corn sowed before anyone else in the district. His voice was often heard first thing in the morning urging someone on. I well remember one warm day I was harrowing in a field called Blake Dale. It was warm, the sun shone, and I was on top song, singing a favourite song of mine: "Where the bee sucks, there suck I." As I sang the horses went slower and slower. We were all in complete harmony, and I had just reached the passage: "On a bat's wing I do fly, I do-ooo fly," when there was a piercing shout from behind me: "Fly you sods, fly!"

The horses shot forward. I had the driving strings hanging loosely round my wrists. I jumped, the sudden jerk by the horses tightened the strings and I tripped and fell on the harrows. The foreman shouted "Whoa" and the horses stopped and then I heard the rest of what he had to say about so-and-so kids who sung their so-and-so horses to sleep, then off he went. But I am sure that the echoes from the shout are still sounding across the Wolds.

Of course, it became a joke on the farm, but one of the labourers said afterwards that the foreman told him that he had walked up behind me ready to, as he put it, "boot his backside to waken him up," but he was so tickled with "on a bat's back I do fly" that he decided he would shout at us instead. I doubt if he would have "booted my backside." He was not a vicious chap, keen yes: if there was a drop of blood in a stone he would have it. Besides I was now coming up to sixteen and past the "booting stage." I never, after I left, worked with a fairer foreman or one who kept a better table.

Wagoners Reserve field day at Mr. Megginson's Fimber Field Farm in 1914 just before the war started. Three of the men in the wagon were members of the Reserve as was also the driver and were all called up at the start of hostilities. The lad sat at the far right of the wagon was on his "first year off" and is still happily with us in our village. The lady driving the pony and trap is Mrs. Megginson and the three children on the wagon are hers.

Sacks of corn loaded ready for market and "Wag" ready for the off.

CHAPTER FOURTEEN

Horses always came first, no matter the nature of a horseman; be he pigheaded, nasty-natured or a damn good fellow, his horses had to be fed and watered before he went for his own food. One of the first jobs on entering the stables during Winter when the horses were kept in the stables all the time was to take them to the pond to drink. Come rain, snow or frost, the youngest lads had to take the horses they were helping to look after to the pond two at a time.

With snow on the ground, we couldn't see the edge of the pond. The water would be frozen. One of the horses would want to go further into the water and start to smash the ice with its front feet. Old Tinker had a smashing time. I would have hold of his halter rope with one hand, the other holding Bob who couldn't care less about a drink and wanted to get back to the warmth of the stable; so did I!

Tinker would splash me with ice cold water, trying to break the ice. It would be nice if we could turn them out and let them drink their fill and then return. It's been tried. There is always the odd one that wants a walk across the grass field beyond the pond, no matter what the weather, and it's no fun either chasing after a horse in the snow, so we would lead them out and lump it. But I could never understand why we had to get up in the middle of Winter at five o'clock and have breakfast at twenty to six when it was dark until seven a.m. Still, that was the way our forefathers had done it and the farmer was the last person to alter such a tradition.

Hired lads could so easily be spoilt! "Hey there lad, wake up. Thou wants to get hold of that fork and get them hosses mucked out and get some more chaff and choppy into the bins." Day-dreaming was a luxury to be enjoyed after you had finished at night.

Choppy did I say? It was made of oat straw usually. It could be made of any straw but oat was the best, and if a few forkfuls of clover could be added to it, it made a good mix and the horses loved it. But there was one snag to making it; the straw had to be fed by hand into a narrow wooden trough on the cutter so that it came into the roller feeding the knives which were fastened to a wheel that was spinning round at a fair speed. The wheel was turned by hand, and it was too heavy for us young lads to turn so the senior horsemen had to do it themselves, so you can bet that it was done only when the horses were working hard and wanted tempting to eat.

More oats was not the answer, for as any horseman knew, give a horse extra oats in with its feed of chaff and unless the next feed had as many or more oats in it, the horse stalled and would refuse to eat, and then the feeder had a problem on his hands for a few weeks. The balance of corn had to be kept the same. With a nag that did very little work, it didn't matter, but with one pulling a plough or a set of harrows it had to be eating regularly. It was a temptation to use the drugs that every horseman knew that he shouldn't, but it was a matter of pride that you should have good fit horses, well groomed and with a shine on their coats.

All the corn was drilled and growing nicely and the turnip seed all sown. Some of the turnips were ready for hoeing, one of the jobs mostly done by piecework in days gone by when the labourers, if they had any children, would take a field to hoe at so many pence per chain, share the rows out amongst them and it then became a family job. The seed was sown in a continuous line and the hoer had to chop out the surplus and leave one plant every nine inches. If he went too fast he would either leave more than one plant or chop the lot and leave and eighteen-inch gap, which meant a drop in his piece rate.

A man with a family would have the wife hoeing as well, and they would push on with the hoeing and leave tufts of six or seven plants for the children following them to single out. The children would be doing it before they went to school from six in the morning, and when they came more in the afternoon there would be plenty of rows waiting for them to do until supper time.

Sometimes school was missed for a week during turnip-hoeing time. Len told me that he always was off school during that period. He told me that his mother was helping his Dad in the field when she started to have her eighth baby, so she went home and Len went into the village two miles away to fetch Mrs Pitcher. She was the village midwife; the only training those old midwives ever had as experience, having their own children. When they got back to his mother she had had her baby and was making a cup of tea for them.

All women went turnip-hoeing for their bairns or for a little extra in the house. The wives of some of the farm labourers were more money-conscious than their husbands and grasped every opportunity to get more money for miserly reasons. Some were so greedy they would dole out the husband's pocket money. They seldom had more than one or two children, and were thin-lipped women, mean looking.

I don't think it is possible for a man to be as miserly mean as a miserly mean woman who, as old Bob used to say, would skin a flea for its hide. It is strange how often these women got either little men they could push around or a big hulk that they seemed to be able to intimidate around.

There were two cottages together at Sammy's and one could hardly imagine two more different families. In one were Totty and his wife. She was a happy-go-lucky piece of woman, with a heart as big as herself and a family who adored her. The girls were in service and the lads on farms except for one of each still at school, but they all filled the cottage up when they had time off. Us young lads from the farm were just as welcome. It was: "Come in son, if you can find a place sit down." It seemed to me to be a cluttered up sort of spot, but they loved to talk about the old times and existing on twelve shillings a week and how the old folks used to exist.

I remember her telling me about her Dad. He was turned 65 when the Lloyd George five shillings a week pension started, but still working on the farm, and the first week he got his pension the farmer knocked it off his wage. When Totty was doing piecework she was always by his side, and the lads used to pull his leg about walking home hand in hand. Later they got a house in Driffield and Totty went to work on the aerodrome. They were one of the happiest couples I ever met.

Their next door neighbours I remember as being just the reverse and Jack saying: "I've had patches all over my trousers except the pockets. She never gives me owt to put in to wear them out! When it comes to getting wed some of us has to back losers. We had one bairn years ago but I've hardly had chance of another once since, but then she keeps me clean and feeds me well, so what odds."

Harvest came around once more. It was a nice dry time this year and we got on well, but I was still not allowed to drive four horse in the reaper. Charley the blacksmith had left us. He was sent to work as a blacksmith at one of the munition factories. His skill was of more importance there than shoeing horses and repairing machinery, so he was sadly missed when one of the reapers broke down.

I don't think Charley minded though. He was moving from twenty-five shillings a week to double that, and his neighbour Jim had also gone to work on the new aerodrome that was being made in Driffield, almost doubling his wage of a pound a week with Sammy. We were still getting some soldiers released on farm work, so the "opening out" of the cornfields went on, the stooking got done just the same, and the corn was led.

I had a wagon and two horses of my own that harvest. I was growing and toughening up, but still only weighed about 90 lbs although I was strong. Wag was getting morose and bad to deal with and was inclined to drop off to sleep any moment and wake up suddenly and blast anyone near him as though it was their fault until the foreman told him he couldn't burn candle at both ends; if he did, he would have no wick left. I found out later what he meant. I was always asking questions and one of the soldiers explained it one night. I learnt a lot the next few months.

Martinmas came again. Another year had gone, but what's a year when you are sixteen? It was the same procedure as the previous year: Wag first, then the rest in peck order to collect their wages from Sammy, except this year I was not the last, young Len followed me. "Now Harry, let me see, how much do you want?" and he grinned as he remarked: "Let's see, have you been a good lad this year?" then he said: "Are you staying on another year with me?" Real sugary. "No," was my reply, "I want a change on to a bigger farm."

"Now look here my boy, I'll give you as much to stay as anybody else offers you." I still refused. He then said: "I tell you what, Harry, I like you and you know I am not married so I've no family. Stay with me, you might be better off one day." Yeh, I thought, tell me the old old story, and it flashed through my mind, my Grandad saying: "Don't ever wait for a dead man's money. Old Squire kept three of us on his spot for years with promises, then he left us four pounds each and we had been the poorest paid in the parish."

I said I wanted a change. It wasn't that I didn't like him, it was a bigger place I wanted to be at. So he paid me my ten pounds ten shillings, and as I turned to go he said: "Look here Harry, if ever you are stuck and want help, call on me." I was sixteen years old and had been working two years and I thought "I'm a man now, let me get off the spot," but a number of years later when I wrote for a reference, it made me think about it once more when I got his reply. But then if I had stayed with him I would have missed an awful lot of good times and it might not have worked out. I walked out and I didn't see him again for thirty years. I called once at his home and he made quite a fuss of me, but he was then a miserable old man.

£10, 10 shillings. What a lot of money. There were the tailor's bill to pay, washing, shirts and socks to pay for and I did want a bike, but when

I had finished paying back my borrowings from my Dad, a pound just would not buy one. Then came hirings day at Driffield and all the farm workers in the district met there. Those who were already hired for the next year were either in the various pubs or walking the main street end to end, but the rest of us stood in the Market Place waiting for a foreman or farmer who would be sauntering round as though valuing cattle, to come and ask if you wanted hiring.

I had my back to the Cross Keys when Ted came up to me. I knew him by sight. He was the foreman/hind on one of the larger Wolds farms. A bluff, hearty type of chap, he was known as a good foreman who knew his job and, most important, kept a good table. Whenever farm lads got together the first two things they asked one another were: "What's the boss (meaning the foreman) like?" and "What sort of a table does he keep?" The horses and the rest came later, and the farmer himself rarely came into it on the big farms.

Ted met all the requirements, so I thought: "We are in business Harry lad." His first words were: "Have you got hired yet my lad?" "No," I replied. "How about coming to our spot then up at Warren Farm? How much do you want for the year?" "£16 and a 5/- fest." I knew it would be turned down flat — it was. Ted said: "I want a Thoddy's lad and I will give thou £15 and 5/- fest and not a penny more." "Right," I said. "That's it then. Here's your 5/- fest and mind you are on the spot December 1st and bring your box."

Every hired man had his box. For the first year or two it was usually a metal one, just enough to hold a change of clothing, Sunday suit, etc. Every hardware store used to keep them in stock, but I haven't seen one for years. Then, as the lad got older and could afford to buy one, he went to the local joiner and he made you a wooden one for ten shillings or less. The bosses liked to see the boxes arrive with the new lads. There was less chance of them "running away" when they had a box to consider, if they didn't like the place.

This was not unusual happening if the lad had come from a good distance away. He would work for a week or two, and then one Saturday night he would go out for the evening and not return. In days gone by it didn't matter much as there were always a number of lads who had not got hired at the Martinmas hirings and were only too pleased to fill any vacancy.

CHAPTER FIFTEEN

On December 1st I was on the farm for six o'clock tea. Most of us were fresh faces, though some had stayed on for another year. The waggoner or "Wag" was one of them. Herbert was his christian name. He was a chap who was master of his job and could control and hold the respect of the rest of the staff, and there were one or two who took some holding. But to us youngsters he was the best chap I ever worked under. He had been a wag for a number of years and was still a young man. His one object was to get enough money to start a farm of his own. He had made a good start by courting the eldest daughter of a small farmer, and by the Lady Day of the next year he married and went as hind on one of the large farms on the Wolds, feeding up to ten lads. This was the best way to make extra money on the farm, but one had to have a wife who wasn't frightened of work and Herbert got just that.

During the depression years of the 1920's he got the offer of a farm to rent. It was a start and he grabbed it. Our paths did not cross again after he left for another 45 years, when by a coincidence we both retired to the same village. He had just one regret in a life he had enjoyed: they had no children.

It was a hard Winter that year and there was very little work for the horses to do. The land was far too hard for ploughing and they were all in the stables "eating their heads off" and so blessed fit that one could hardly lead them out to the pond for watering. As the pond was frozen over each morning one of us used to break the ice at the edge. But some of the horses very quickly learnt how to break the ice by smashing it with their forefeet and sending cold icy water on to your trouser bottoms, a most uncomfortable start to the day.

There was a terrific blizzard one night, causing huge drifts everywhere, and the shepherd reported that his ewes had made for the hedgeside for shelter and the snow had drifted over and covered them up. It was a long hedge and they were covered up anywhere along a length of about six hundred yards, so it meant starting at one corner and digging right to the other one with not too much time to spare or we would find half of them suffocated. Then we had to get them moving, pushing and pulling to get circulation going. They were a prize flock and due for lambing in a few weeks time. However, we got them moving and down to the home pasture which was sheltered by a plantation and the shepherd was able to give them some extra food in the cribs.

Then we turned ourselves to the mundane job of clearing the stackyard of all the loose straw and chaff etc. left from the last few times we had been threshing. It had rotted and was a nuisance and an eyesore, so foreman Ted decided now was the time to move it. "Right Thoddy, get four horses yoked to the snowplough." It was always left just inside the plantation on the roadside. All the farms on the high Wolds had a plantation round three sides, leaving the south side open, and there was always a terrific view across the countryside.

We had to cut a cart width through the snow down the lane as far as the horse pasture just so that we could lead the straw and muck into the field. So off the horses went, plunging and struggling through the deep drift pulling the heavy wooden plough behind them, leaving a path seven foot wide and sides which depended on the depth of the drift.

The next morning it was cold and frosty, and at nearly seven o'clock, Wag came through into Thoddy's stable and said: "We're clearing stackyard today. Tell your lad (that was me) to yoke up a cart to lead it down to horse pasture. My lad Tom and Dave will have the other two carts. Two labourers can help to load and two can be in the field to spread it about."

Quite often where a farm had a competent wagoner such as we had in Herbert, the running of the labour force at such times as this was left to him. "OK, lad," said Thoddy, "take Tidy out. She hasn't done anything for over a week. She is getting so damn fat and frisky, it's time she had a go." My heart sank. Tidy, of all the six horses he and I did between us, she was the most stubborn, and if she wanted to go her way nothing would stop her.

She was fit and fat, but refused year after year to have a foal. The previous Summer when the entire came on his weekly visit she carried on so much that the entire's groom refused to entertain her again. By jove, the present day's women's lib would have loved her! She had a mouth as hard as iron. You could pull at the reins as hard as you could but she just turned her head to the side you were pulling and off she went on her own way, although at times you could yoke her to implements with other horses or to a cart on her own and one couldn't wish to be with a nicer mare. But after a few days idling, there was no holding her.

However, orders were orders, and we didn't argue with either Wag or Thoddy on such matters as not liking to take Tidy because she can be awkward to handle or, to put it plainly, that I was frightened of her. No, you put the harness on her for yoking into a cart, took her out, prancing and showing off, in the snowy yard, got her yoked into the cart then to the stackyard to be loaded with the straw and muck, hoping that she would calm down. Strangely enough she did, leading three or four loads down to the pasture down the narrow cutting and then the last load before dinner.

We tipped the load up, set off for home, then just through the gate one of the labourers threw his fork into the empty cart. Tidy jumped a yard in the air and set off at the gallop. I tried to hold her but I might as well have pulled at the back end of the cart. She got the bit and kept going. I knew what would happen, there was no room for me to get out of the way, the walls of snow were too high. At last one of her forefeet caught my legs and down I went, a second's job, but I remember thinking as I was going down: "How on earth will they bury me with all this snow on the ground?" and "I wonder if my Mother will come to the funeral," and a host of other things, so I will now let Frank take up the story.

"Yes, Harry lad. Me and Sid rushed up to thou. Thou was laid on slush and muck and Sid says: 'Is he dead?' I said I deant know but that wheel went over his napper and by the looks of that blood it's fetched his lug off, and I spoke to thou and thou didn't answer, so Jim said: 'Poor little sod,' and we were still looking at thou when boss shouted: 'Never mind him! Come and look after the mare before she hurts herself!'"

She had galloped further on and run one wheel on to the snowbank and overturned herself and the cart, so she was laid struggling to get overend but held down by the cart shafts. Someone had to sit on her head whilst someone else undid the harness and loosened her collar so that she could get up. Then came my turn for removal.

It was dark when I woke up, I groaned or moved or something and a voice which seemed to come from a long way off — it was Thoddy with whom I slept — said: "Oh, thou is still alive then! How does thou feel?" "I don't know," I said. "Oh well, we will soon find out. It's getting up time!" By then Wag shouted: "Hey up, let's be having you." That was the regular call every morning at 4.30 in Summer and 5 o'clock in Winter, and everybody jumped out of bed except me.

I found that I could move my right side but the left one seemed stuck and my head felt queer. Wag came round to the bedside: "Now lad," he said, "can't thou get out of bed?" "No," I replied. "I seem a bit stuck." "I'm not surprised, seeing the mess thou was in when we brought thou in and put thou to bed, I thought we were going to have to swill thou to get blood and muck off. Better stop there a couple of days. I'll tell them downstairs and the lasses will bring thy breakfast to bed."

Later in the morning Ted the foreman came up to see me and told me that they hadn't got a doctor because the roads to Driffield, Sledmere and Langtoft were all completely blocked and besides I was still alive because I was breathing and besides, get a couple of days over and I would be all right again. The only bit of sympathy I got was when Mrs. Ted (she was a lovely woman) brought me some breakfast and sat and helped me to get it to my mouth.

Two days later I was up and I took stock of my aches and pains. The steel rim of the wheel had travelled right down the left side of me, grazing my ear and the side of my face, travelled over my shoulder and down my arm, then along the left leg bruising and cutting the fleshy part of the thigh and then to the foot where it had pulled my boot off even though it was laced, but did no damage to the foot itself except for a bit of stiffness.

I had been lucky! But my left arm was hanging by my side and I couldn't lift it up, so after a few days, when the roads were open and the snowploughs had got through most of the main roads, I set off for Driffield and the doctor. Dr. Keith soon told me what was wrong: a nasty flesh rent tore the muscle from the bone, nothing we could do except put it into a sling and move it as little as possible for a few weeks. "Come back in a fortnight's time."

So off I went back and told Ted the news. "Oh, that's all right, nothing to do this weather, get it proper better." But the snow went and the sun got warmer and the land was ready for working and Ted was wanting the Spring corn sowing and one of his horsemen was kicking his heels doing nothing and, as he put it, "eating his blasted head off." But I was hired for the year and there was nothing else he could do but feed me and wait until the doctor said right, and I was still having difficulty lifting the arm.

However, another week or two passed and Dr. Keith said: "I think you can start now doing a bit of light work, but don't overdo it or we will be back to or worse than when we started." So off I went back to the farm and told Ted what the doctor had said. Ted brisked up: "Silly old clot, what's he know about light work? It's all light work on a farm. Get your dinner if there's any left and then get a couple of horses and get off up to Old Sledmere and start harrowing. There is a set of harrows there. Get a move on, we are behind already." So off I went. My lazy days were over, my injuries were forgotten and the following day I was up again at five a.m., and as Thoddy said: "It's a good job thou is right handed!"

Lambing time was over and the lambs were a few weeks old. It was time for castration and tail cutting, a job the shepherd and his lad, assisted by a labourer, always did. So all the lambs were drawn out in the field and the job started. The lad caught the lamb, handed it to the labourer who held it with its back to his chest, two legs in each hand, then the shepherd would cut two thirds of its tail off and castrate the male lambs. It was a messy job, but all you wanted was a sharp knife and no feelings whatsoever.

Then they got an early lamb, a bit stronger than the others, and it struggled more and loosened one hind leg catching the shepherd in the face. Shep was a short-tempered chap at any time and slashed at the tail with some force. Another kick diverted the knife blade into his arm, blood spurted, and it was panic stations. Nobody had the faintest idea how to stop the bleeding, but the spurting stopped. Shep felt faint so he sat on the seat of the low pony float they had for moving nets and posts in the sheepfold.

A few minutes later he fell into the body of the float. The other two then decided that the best plan would be to take him to hospital four miles away. He was dead when they got there — for a trained first-aider it would have been just a nasty cut and he would have dealt with it. No wonder that when the opportunity came I threw myself into first aid work and kept it up for the rest of my working life and with more restrained enthusiasm for the next fifteen years. The St. John Ambulance Brigade is a worthy organisation.

CHAPTER SIXTEEN

The war was still on and labour scarce. Turnip-hoeing time was almost here, then muck leading. There were two big foldyards to be cleaned out, and by then it would be harvest. So the gaffer applied for and got four soldiers to help out, four as diverse characters as you could meet anywhere.

One was G.A.H. His home was near Nottingham and his father was a schoolmaster. George's trade was a ladies' silk stocking maker, so of course he got all the ribald comments, but a nicer fellow never walked across those Driffield Wolds, and as a man he gained more respect the longer he stayed with us.

A.G.G. came from Herefordshire and had been a farm worker as a young fellow but moved into a town job just before the war started and so he had been called up. Arthur had a small chip on his shoulder. He could do the job all right but resented having to do farm work on soldiers' pay. However, as time went on, his attitude became: "I'm better off here than at the Front," and he settled down.

The next one, I don't even remember his name but we will call him Tim, was the one misfit of all the men were were drafted onto farms that I came into contact with. I remember that first night with us. It was a regular thing for most of us to go across to our bedroom at the same time, so the fresh chaps came with us. It was a large bedroom or a small dormitory, call it which you like, but there were six double beds in it and one single and two double beds just off it.

We all got undressed and tumbled into bed, but Tim wanted to get washed. Wag explained that us lads were only allowed two washes a day, before breakfast and before tea, and if he wanted an extra wash he would have to go to Driffield; water was too scarce up there. Tim sank back on the bed, opened his kit bag and took out a little bag, got undressed, took off his shirt and put a pair of pyjamas on. Most of us had never seen them before and a howl of laughter went up when he stood in his pyjamas before getting into bed.

Oh dear! Tim burst his bonds: "Bloody savages, going to sleep in their stinking shirts. The last unwashed race of turnip mashers!" It made no difference to our enjoyment of the moment. Farmworkers of those days accepted the conditions as a part of life. Our fathers and forefathers had lived the same life under probably worse conditions, and if one went back only sixty years before then, one would have found that the majority of people lived fairly rough.

Three days later, with his hands badly blistered through using a hoe, he got an excuse note from the "guvnor" and departed back to barracks.

The fourth one was T.S.L., Thomas Stanley L. We called him Tommy. He was a little runt of a chap. A Cockney born in Peckham Rye, with two passions in life: one was women and the other horses. He had only been with us a week before he asked Ted if he could look after two horses, one of the old horses that had been pushed out of the stables by an intake of fresh young ones and the other a "half-legged" one, so called because it was a cross between a hunter stallion and a Clydesdale mare. Most of the Wolds farmers had one or two for use either on the land or for going to market with in one of the light carts in winter. This one was called Cobby, a black gelding as proud a horse as one could wish to see.

Tommy was in his element. Every spare moment, when he was not chasing after some female, was spent grooming Cobby and Tinker, and as for the farm work, it was no effort. He liked it, and the jobs that he couldn't do someone else did.

There was now a diversion on the farm. Ted's family were growing up and he had some of the bonniest lasses one could wish to meet. They were aged about eighteen downwards, seven of them. To us lads on the farm they were same as the daughters of the labourers, or those in the "big house," strictly taboo. But Tommy was different and he started to cast his roving eye on the older ones, but Ted also kept his eye on them. Like a miser with his gold he noticed the movements and took steps — but let Tommy tell you as he told us in the bothy that evening.

"Old Ted came across to me in the stackyard and says: 'Look Tommy, me and Charlie the beastman are doing a little job in the foldyard. I want you to come and give us a hand.' So off we go into this loose box and there were two bull calves so Ted says to me 'We are going to castrate them. Have you seen it done?' I says no, so him and Charlie gets hold of one, slings it on its back with a bag over its eyes and its legs tied up. Charlie gets his knife out of his pocket, two cuts, Ted reached him what he called the clams, threw two things to one side, and it was done. They then did the other. I was near sick by then. When they finished Ted looks at me and said 'It's just as easy to do a chap like you as it is to do them and if I see or hear of you messing about near my lasses that's what will happen to you'."

Tommy was scared stiff. He said: "I'm sure the old blighter meant it," and when some of the chaps started reminiscing, Thoddy said: "Yes, I remember my uncle telling me about a chap. He was one of the old cattle drover gang. He had been making himself a nuisance and the servant lasses were getting frightened of going back to their places in the dark, so some of the chaps grabbed him one night and castrated him." "Yes," said old Arthur, "He was the backdoor handyman and looked after the wants of the 'big house.' When I was a young fellow we had a spot of bother with some of the gangs of labourers who were making the Driffield - Market Weighton line, and it got that no woman was safe at any time, so some of the men from the village got hold of the worse offender and did the same. There was no more of it — drastic justice but it worked."

The author, Martinmas 1916, in his first new suit, tailor-made by Fred Hornby, of Driffield. The watch chain held an Ingersoll half crown watch.

It stopped Tommy dead in his tracks as regards our girls. He wasn't risking it. Not that Ted would have been so drastic, knowing him, but he was a powerfully built man and I am sure Tommy would have had a rough time if he had ignored the warning.

There was another one in the field also, George. He fell for the second oldest, a really good-looker, well-built and with a nice nature, but he wasn't having any of it there either. He wasn't going to have a ladies' silk stocking maker in the family and everybody laughing at him. Poor George, his reply was: "When I get back to civvy street I shall make more money per week than he earns in a month. There are not a lot of chaps with my skill." That was the end, but he wrote a letter or two to me after the war when he got home and then it stopped. I think that his heart was still on the Driffield Wolds.

Tommy was a great story-teller, and if he could get an audience his stories of Cockney life were great fun to us who had only read of London and had no great wish to go. It seems by what I remember, that his father was a dealer in anything, horses included, and did a bit of hawking. He used to tell us that when father used to come home in the evening the rully would be emptied into the front room and the horse taken down the hallway through the kitchen and stabled in the backyard, and the reverse in the morning.

He was a character and he got on well with everyone. I got a letter from him after he was demobbed with his visiting card enclosed (which as a matter of interest I still have) saying that Thomas Stanley Lill, Cartage Contractor, heavy and light haulage, Stables, etc., were in Peckham, London. He told me in his letter that he called the first horse that he bought Cobby. Those soldiers-cum-farmworkers did a lot to open our dust-covered eyes to another world.

Another accident happened. This time it was Jim, one of the labourers who helped in the sheepfold (we had got another shepherd). He was putting a sheepnet up across a part of a 90-acre field to keep the sheep in separate clocks, and it entailed using an iron gablock, a heavy bar with a pointed end which you drove into the ground by brute force. A part of the lower end of it was square and the rest of it round for way handling. It was a fairly heavy thing. You drove it into the ground a time or two depending on how hard the ground was, then put the pointed end of the stake in the hole and hammered it down firm with the squared part of the gablock. Each stake was placed so many strides apart, and then the sheepnet was fastened onto them.

Jim was doing the job and just as he crashed it down into the ground, one of the sheep bumped him. Thump, the gablock went straight through his boot, then his foot, and the point went through the sole. He shouted to the other two who were working nearby. They came over and surveyed the foot. With a typical country phlegmatic approach, one said: "That's nasty Jim. We will have to get the gablock out." So out it came. Blood squirted out of Jim's boot. "Thou had better get thyself home and see the doctor and get the bleeding stopped," was the advice given.

They were working in the "old ninety," and Jim's cottage was one of two at the crossroads at the far corner from them. So Jim set off. His two mates kept an eye on him and he had got nearly home when he fell. As he didn't get up his mates went across to him. "He seems to have passed out," said Bill, "we had better carry him in." This they did and laid him on the couch.

Mrs. Jim, a sturdy type, took charge and Bill started to tell her what had happened and remarked: "By gum, it was bleeding badly, but thank goodness it has stopped." Poor Jim, he was nearly drained dry. His wife set off to walk to Langtoft, four miles away, to get the doctor. He was on his round, so she set off to intercept him if possible, which fortunately she did.

The doctor was in his pony cart, motor cars hadn't reached Langtoft yet, and after a good two hours they got to the cottage, nearly too late, but however pull round he did after months off work. But oh, if they had only taken that boot off quickly and put some padding on the foot and tied it on firmly over the wound and carried him on one of their sheep bars across the field, the damage would have been halved.

The cottage next to Jim's had been empty a couple of months, and with Jim off, another labourer was a necessity and that was when Frank came to us. He had worked on farms in Holderness for many years but wanted to be back again on the Wolds. He and his wife were the nicest couple one could meet, not averse to letting anyone seeing their affection for one another. They had quite a large family, all but one of whom were away working.

One of the lads started to work with us right away. He was the same age as myself and the weekends would see their small cottage filled to overflowing as the girls brought their young men and we lads from the farm landed to the cottage. We flooded the place and Mrs. Frank would be pushing bacon sandwiches and fruit pies at us. She was a wonderful woman. She lived to be over a hundred and no one was ever more worthy of reaching it.

The whole family went to an ordinary village school, and the eldest boy joined the navy at the beginning of the war at eighteen and finished his service career as a Wing Commander in the R.A.F., in charge of an R.A.F. station forty years later. Her father used to come and stay with them quite frequently. I remember him as an elderly, very upright, tall old gentleman who used to tell us lads stories about his job.

He had been a gamekeeper as had his father before him. He had lost an eye through a skirmish with some poachers in the 1890's at a period when the only fresh meat a lot of country folks got came from the Squire's or his Lordship's pampered game. They paid a gamekeeper to rear and keep an eye on them and, most important, to make sure that no poachers came near them. The best way was for a gamekeeper to get a name for being trigger-happy. As the old chap said to us once: "His Lordship said to me 'Fire at them and tumble on the ground immediately, and then if you hit anybody say that your gun went off when you tripped up'."

They were never short of meat when he was staying with them. He used to go out every night with his snickles. There were a lot of hares up there in those days, and Pop knew the job. He was inclined to be sceptical about staying all your life with one family (as employers) on the promise or suggestion that "you will be all right when you retire" or alternately "when I die you won't be forgotten." "Yes," he told us, "when I got too old to do the job we had to get out of our cottage to make way for the new gamekeeper and live in a miserable little spot in the village that nobody else would have, and then we lost mother and now I spends my time going round and staying with my bairns."

CHAPTER SEVENTEEN

At last I got a bicycle, after wanting one for years. Dad lent me three pounds, but I had to pay him back at Martinmas when I got my pay. I had now gone up to eighteen pounds for the year, and after walking to and from the farms for three years I could now join the other lads and get round the other East Riding villages, or on fine Sundays go over to Hull for the day. As Dave, one of the other lads, lived just outside Beverley, we often went home together.

I remember one Sunday evening, we stayed talking to some girls in his village until after 10 p.m. then set off back to Warren fifteen miles away, an hour's easy run. We had gone two miles when Dave's bike punctured. We walked to the next village. Dave was sure that a chap he knew would lend him his bike to get back. Dave banged at the door and the front bedroom window opened: "What the hell do you want?" "Will you lend me your bike, Walt, we've punctured and we have a heck of a long way to go." "No!" blasted out Walt. "I have a long way to go in the morning at five o'clock, so clear off and let me get some sleep." "Right," said Dave, "I will leave my bike in your front garden 'til next Sunday. Get it repaired for me."

The window banged down so we decided that we would both ride my bike, one on the saddle and one on the crossbar. Another mile on and, bang, mine punctured — that Driffield to Beverley road was a rough one in those days. There was no tarmacadam then, and a cyclist used to carry a piece of wood to poke out the mud from the mudguards in wet weather. So we set off to walk pushing the bike. We arrived back at the farm just as the other lads were getting up, at 4.30 a.m. It was a long day!

There was a war on. Not that anyone in our remote area noticed it, but an innovation as regards farming came on the scene, double furrowed ploughs instead of the single furrow and two horses. There were two furrows and three horses, so that instead of ploughing one acre a day, one man did two, and on the light, chalky Wolds land, the horses hardly noticed the difference.

A lot of new machinery was coming on to the farms: new reapers with an eight foot cut as against the old six foot cut, and then "it" arrived. Ted, the foreman, had been hinting a while about things getting "wakened up on this spot" and "them there horses crawling about the fields." "Just you wait," he said.

Then one morning it arrived, the thing that was to change the whole face of farming and alter working conditions that had altered little over the years. It was a Fordson tractor. All four wheels were steel, the rear driving wheels having a separate four in a wide circular rim which clamped on to the wheels when it was travelling on the highway and a number of pieces of angle iron which were bolted on when they were required for an extra grip on the land, such as for going up or down some of the hillsides in dales that were worked.

Ted was in his element. Nobody was allowed to drive it but him. A man came from Driffield to teach him all about it, but I think that all he wanted to know was how to start, how to stop and how to make it go faster. When I look back and think of the reception that some of the previous labour-saving machines had received, such as the reaper which did away with scything, and its successor, the binder, which tied the cut corn into nice even sheaves and dropped them in nice even rows so that a gang of men could go into a field and have stooked in a tenth of the time previously taken. Also, when I think of the reception given to the innovation of the first of the threshing machines, all of which had caused near riots, the advent of the tractor, which was to cause the loss of thousands of jobs and alter the whole of farming life and methods for ever, caused barely a ripple.

The older hands regarded it as a new-fangled thing that would be a twenty minute wonder, and as far as they were concerned it would never affect them and, as Frank put it, they will never get one to slash hedges. Ha, ha — they go round the field nowadays slashing and trimming hedges as neat and tidy as the old-time labourer ever did, and they do a heavy four-year growth in hours that once took weeks to do by hand.

As for the horsemen, well, as Wag put it, they will always want horses, if only to tow the blamed things in when they break down. Poor foreman Ted, the indignity of it all when his beloved Fordson stuttered to a stop one day and one of us horselads had to tow him back to the farm and wait for the arrival of the mechanic. But Ted never faltered in his belief in the future of the tractor, although he finally had to hand over the driving to someone else.

Maurice was a lad who had come to work on a farm instead of going into the army. His father was a wool merchant in Bradford and owned a motor car which Maurice had driven, so he jumped at the chance to drive the tractor — he disliked having anything to do with horses.

Ted was a pioneer in the use of tractors in the East Riding but even he could not have foreseen that within the lifetime of one of his young hired lads the talk of the farm lads of the future would be about the relative merits of Fords or Internationals against JCB's or Ferguson, with maybe someone butting in with the merits of those new Russian tractors with their special heating — Ted would have loved it all. Unfortunately he left us quite a few years ago, but I still see a lot of his family about.

The year rolled on, Herbert the waggoner had got married and left us to go hinding on another farm. His place was taken by George. He had been discharged from the forces through wounds: a piece of shrapnel had sliced two fingers and a piece of his hand off. The soldiers who had been helping us, Tommy, George and Arthur, had been recalled to barracks and were re-training for the "big push" of 1917/18.

The various agricultural boards were getting into their stride and dictating what the farmer could grow and where and telling experienced people to do things that a "first-year-off" lad could have told them was a stupid idea, such as the order given to us at Warren to sow the field known as "Old Sledmere" down with barley.

Old Sledmere was 150 acres, and of that about a third was so infested with rabbits which had burrowed into the hillsides and deep into the land that it was dangerous for any horse to walk across it. Plus there was the fact that corn had been sown on it at various times previously, and as soon as it got to any height, the rabbits just ate it off. But orders are orders and no-one dared go against them, so it was sown with barley, that part of it that could be worked, and the same thing happened again, so that at harvest, there was not as much grain gathered as had been sown.

I pass the field now very often and it is a showpiece for modern farming. Myxomatosis took the rabbits away, deeper ploughing and harrowing with the big new tractors gave plenty of tilth, and with the right fetilisers there is now a hundred acres of the field with a really good crop each year. The tractors charge up and down the hills where once the horses struggled to work and the men could not hold the ploughs upright on the steep hillsides.

It was threshing day. I hated them, as every young lad did. We always got the rotten job of carrying the chaff and the pulls away from the machine, a dusty, lung-filling job that left you with sore eyes and a cough that lasted until you had cleared all the filth that you had breathed in. I had carried the chaff all the previous day, but today Wag, Thoddy, and Dave were delivering the threshed corn by wagon to Driffield so we were the corn carriers short, and there was only one married labourer who was young enough and strong enough to do the job.

"Right," said Ted, "you can carry corn Harry lad." "No," I replied, "I wasn't hired to carry corn and I'm not going to for eighteen pounds for the year and I am still only eighteen." Ted was stumped. He knew I was right, and I had seen some of the results of young lads trying to be men or being forced to by a bullying farmer, before they were grown up or strong enough.

When one comes to think that a bag of beans from the machine weighs 20 stones, wheat was 18, barley 16 and oats 12, those lads were easy to pick out with their hunched or mis-shapen backs which got worse as the years went by. I remember old Bob saying to me on my first year off: "Don't ever be a clever devil and start carrying corn before you are strong enough, and that doesn't want to be until you're twenty-two, and if they try to make you carry it, accidentally drop a bag or two in an awkward spot; they will soon take you off. I got this lopsided shoulder through doing just that."

However, Ted threatened, then cajoled and finally persuaded me to carry the corn. As he put it, it's nobbut oats and you are only carrying it into wagons for delivery to station. "Do it until dinner-time, then the others will be back." So I carried it for the first time, and, I told myself during the morning, the very last time. I was certainly not going to risk injury.

The time was fast approaching when a pig-headed farmer who had been used to treating his hired lads as near slaves as to what they could or had to do, would have to alter his attitude to labour and to human rights. There were still many places where the union man was not allowed to enter the farm from off the roadside, but they were now getting a lot of members and the farmworkers union badge with its "speed the plough" motto and a print in enamel of a plough was now being openly worn by farm hands.

A revolution in farming was on hand, but it was not so much the unions as that thing that Ted was so fussy about, the tractor. None of us could imagine how its descendants would take over in just a few years in the future. But there was one thing the unions had succeeded in doing, and that was the lowering of the weekly hours from seventy-two to fifty — we now didn't start work until 7 a.m. and had Saturday afternoons off.

I quite well remember the comments that were passed when the finishing time was lowered from 6 p.m. to 5 p.m. on Saturdays, such as "five short days and a little bit and all for the same money, but I'll watch none of them get paid until I've had my tea on Saturday night."

That first break in the farm lad's working hours must have been a bitter pill for a lot of the small farmers who were usually the worst to work for, mainly because they were, on the whole, scratting to save every penny they handled in the hope that one day they would be able to go onto a bigger farm. Their lads were never starved of food but broth, into which you were supposed to put plenty of dry bread, was an everyday meal along with plenty of turnip and potatoes and the large piece of beef, the whole lot boiled in the big pan hanging from the trivet.

To save a few more coppers the cut would be the cheapest the butcher could produce and sometimes so fat and gristly as to be past eating or certainly beyond chewing. But as the lads on that sort of place used to say "We does same as bullocks, swallow it now and chew it later." There was never a shortage of pies, even if some of them were rather short of filling.

When the Saturday afternoon off came into being, the hired men had a real grievance. They were hired as horsemen, beastmen or shepherds and as such had to feed their stock at the weekends by the terms of their hirings, which meant that from the end of September until the next May when stock could be turned out into the fields, each night and weekends they had to feed the stock as usual, so they were still tied down to the farm.

If there were any cows, and most places had two or three, the poor beastman had to milk them twice a day, 365 days a year. Most farmers nowadays get their milk out of nice clean bottles. Milking at the weekend is overtime and no-one is keen to do it. Long gone are the days when by dint of scraping and doing extra work whenever possible and finally getting a hundred pounds together, a man could start farming on a small place, probably on one of the large estates, and then start it all over again, scrat, save, and maybe if they were lucky get a bigger farm. Then when they were just about worn out with hard work, they died and left it all to someone else — they very rarely made old bones.

CHAPTER EIGHTEEN

Harvest time again, but now I was moving up in the peck order. Instead of being dogsbody, I was driving four horses pulling a Massey Harris binder, probably the easiest job on the harvest field. The horses were yoked two in front of two, and you rode the nearside rear horse, and drove by reins and word of mouth. The saddles were usually fairly comfortable. Of course there were never any stirrups and besides nobody ever wanted them. If the horse you were riding happened to tread into a rabbit hole and fall it could be very awkward with your legs probably still hooked into them.

"Right," said Ted, "no more messing about mowing round the field opening out. Just cut a few square yards with the scythe round the gateway so that we can get into the field, and then we drive round the field with the binder. What bit of corn we waste is nothing compared to the labour we save. Them folks over yonder think we're daft, but they will all be doing it next year."

Sure enough, every farmer did it the following year, but Ted started it. Six times round the field, and then the stookers started, two men taking three rows each. It was remarkable how quickly a field could be finished, and then all that was wanted was a few fine days with sun and breeze and then it could be led.

It was the same harvest that I had another runaway; it was in Old Sledmere field. We had sown it with barley, as per orders, so it had to be reaped, a light crop, half of it eaten off by rabbits. We pulled in with our binders. The field had quite a large dale across one side, too steep to grow anything on, and another side dropped steeply to the roadside. But the part that we were cutting was fairly level, so off we went, four horses all fit and fresh. Two of them could nearly have managed, but four it was: a nice day.

I was content and thinking about nothing in particular when I clapped the ends of the reins together. The four of them shot off like a gun across the field, through the standing corn. My reaper man Jim pushed the lever to put it out of gear and then dropped the reaper points as near to the ground as possible so that if I was thrown off I would not be dragged underneath the machine.

But Tidy, the mare I was riding, was quite a nimble type and she kept her feet and we hit no rabbit holes. Across the field we stormed, across to the roadside fall. That was when we all started to worry, because we all knew that if they started to go down the bank the whole lot would finish at the bottom in one ghastly heap, horses, reaper and myself.

We were almost to the edge, when there was a slackening of speed. Jim had done his job properly. The points protecting the knives, by just skimming the soil, had gathered so much of the standing corn that it had been acting as a top working brake, and four horses could only gallop and pull a dead weight of half a ton or more for a certain distance before either weariness or sense caught up with them. They came to a stop, with the leading pair of horses having their forefeet on the edge, blowing and steaming, but all of them and myself were in one piece, unharmed.

A fortnight later, the field had been cleared, the barley stacked. Officialdom was satisfied: it had made a farmer do what he didn't want to do. The farmer was satisfied: he had proved them wrong. Although he had done as little as he could towards making it a viable crop, he couldn't compete with hundreds of rabbits and a shortage of labour.

Ted's tractor was still only doing the work of a few horses. Its day was to come when its descendants would turn Old Sledmere field upside down and turn it into a productive unit, but now Maurice was driving the tractor and they were hitched to a binder and in a field of their own. His reaper mate had a motor horn fixed to the reaper to sound to tell the driver above all the noise that he had to stop for some breakdown;

usually it was the little gadget that tied the knot in the twine that fastened the corn in the sheaf.

Sometimes on a nice warm day the man on the reaper would get day-dreaming and suddenly wake up and find that his machine was throwing unfastened sheaves out, which meant a lot of bad language when the stookers reached that row and one man had to knock off to fasten a lot of sheaves up with what we called straw bands. They were made by getting a handful of the straight corn, splitting it into both hands, then with a quick twist of the heads together it was split again and put round the loose corn. With another sharp twist we would double the ends under the band. It was a quick, efficient way of tying sheaves, a method that has probably been in use on farms for centuries and was always used when all corn was cut by scythe.

It was good harvest weather and we got on with the reaping. There were three binders going nearly all the day long, and we had a few horses spare to give those pulling the seven foot binder on the heavy wheat field a changeover during the afternoon so as to keep it going a little longer into the night — men never got tired, horses did!

As soon as it was all cut it was all hands to leading it into the stackyard. Ted had planned out where every stack would be put, such as the wheat which was carried from the threshing machine in eighteen stone bags, as near to the granary as possible. Oats were carried in lots of twelve stones, and they were carried the furthest. The barley came in between in sixteens. Peas and beans, which were bagged at twenty stones, were not grown, or very rarely, on the Wold farms.

There were three kinds of stacks that were generally built on the farms, the gable end, built like a house, but with just a little bulge outwards at the eaves, much favoured on the Wolds. It could be made to hold a full day's threshing, or more if it was required to make it bigger in order to finish a field off in one stack.

There was real craft in building a gable-ended stack. The ends had to be plumb; the sides had to belly out at the same time, and every course of sheaves when it came to topping it had to draw in the same distance, and each one had to be laid the same way. As the sheaves were thrown from the binder, the final squeeze as the knot was tied round it gave it a flat side and what we called a "cockle side," where the straw ends bushed out. The flat side was up so that any rain would run off, but the ends were built with the cockle side up, keeping the end plumb to the last sheaf which would finish as a pyramid, 3, 2, 1, the last one at each end being called the "weetie." Why, I don't know.

The second type, the round end stack, was the commonest, as it was easy to make and just right for a half day's threshing. If the straw stack was getting low and the granary was full, the corn could be left in bags until it was wanted. The third stack was the pike. It was probably the more difficult to make but on completion it stood out in a stackyard, and in those days a farm that stood on the side of the road or rail always built two or three for show.

The difference in the pike was that it was round, and the stacker had to start with a base diameter of, say, sixteen feet and by the time he reached the eaves it should be nineteen feet, the whole thing plumb and from whichever side it was looked at, it was equal in its expansion. The stacker of one of those used to get plenty of exercise, because after, at the most, two loads, he would be running down the ladder and taking a distance view of his stack, making sure it was plumb.

At the first sign of a row being out of true he would be pushing or pulling to put it right, and then when he reached the eaves and had to start taking it in to finish the top off, great care was required that it was not brought in too quickly or else he would have a stack or flat roof and the rain would run into the stack instead of running to the eaves and dropping clear. The man who made a good pike was just as much a craftsman on the farm as any engineer in a workshop.

Once more all was safely gathered in and the stacks all ready for thatching, when Ted announced: "No more thatching. Takes too much time up. We'll have one of those wheat stacks threshed and get Frank to put the sheaves in the machine flat so that the straw comes out flat and we will have it bottled." We had got a new gadget that fitted on the machine which tied the straw up into bundles, or bottles as they were generally called, then dropped them in the elevator and to the straw stack.

"Yes," he said, "we will make them just a bit smaller and lay them on the stack top, right side up just as though we were thatching. Start at the eaves and work up and round, fasten them down with binder twine across the top, weighted down with an old plough sock, and they will stand the Winter all right" — and they did. The corn was just as dry as if it had had a first class thatching. The only objection was that on threshing day there was usually a wagon-load of wet straw to take off the stack top in Winter and lead into the foldyard before we could start.

On threshing days there were always two men on the machine, one cutting the bands round the sheaves with a special, slightly curved serrated edge knife cutting each band where it was tied. Every sheaf was tied in the same place on the "cockle side," so as they were forked to him from the stack he knew exactly where its knot was.

He gave it a gentle press with the knife as he passed it to the feeder, at the same time collecting the cut band and holding it in his left hand until he got a handful and then put them all to one side until the stack was finished. Farmers didn't like the bands to go amongst the straw. It could cause complications if a bullock swallowed it.

The feeder would receive the cut sheaf and fan it out and let it drop into the box where the drum was whirling round at a terrific speed. There the whole lot was crushed, but when wheat straw was wanted for thatching he put it in flat, letting it run off his arm level and straight and come out at the back much straighter than the other way You could always tell when there were two good men on the machines, feeding. It produced a continual hum as against a poor feeder who didn't open the sheaves out properly and made the drum thump each time he put one in.

Threshing day was a team job. Each man had his own job and it was no use any one of them trying to push the pace on. If the forkers on the stack who put the sheaves to the cutter went too fast and piled them up against him he would be hampered and his knife would then be a dangerous thing if his cutting arm was knocked by a sheaf. His answer was to "accidentally" let one slip into the drum uncut. Thump, a six inch wide sheaf trying to get through a one inch gap. Bang! Off would fly the big driving belt, and there would be a complete stoppage with the foreman blasting and swearing. The minutes would be lost until the belt was back on and off we would go.

If the feeder tried to make up time and pushed the sheaves through a little faster, the corn would come down into the bags too fast and the corn carriers would be overset. The chaff carriers would not be able to keep "chaff holes" clear and they would get bunged up. The men on the strawstack wouldn't be able to level and stack the straw, and things would grind to a halt. Harmony was essential on threshing day.

There were two foldyards to clean out. We had made a start on one of them in the "quiet" period just before harvest and had made a big heap in one of the fields and the muck we were taking out of the yards now had to be spread over the clover fields that the sheep were at present feeding and then ploughed in and wheat drilled on the top of it.

We always seemed to be having a feud with the shepherd. If we started to spread the manure too early on his clover fields it covered too much of the clover up and his sheep starved, or if it came wet and warm during September it encouraged blow flies and his work was never done.

In the Spring when we wanted to be ploughing that last piece of the turnip field up to get the last of the Spring corn in, he would keep his sheep in it to the last turnip to make sure that the new clover fields for his sheep had got plenty of growth, and of course he would be busy with his ewes and their lambs so he had neither time or temper for anything.

But the yards had to be cleaned out ready for the cattle to come into for the Winter. Leading manure or "muck-plugging" as it was called, was a rotten job even if it was fine weather. The flies were a nuisance and the horses would be kicking and stamping, but if it was wet or raining, well, it beggared belief, hands wet, muckforks wet, trousers, leggings and boots soaked.

Working on a bank of manure four feet or more deep, you cut it out with a triangular-shaped hay knife in breadths three feet wide and took it down to ground level then started at the top again. Every forkful had to be dug out and thrown into the cart until it was piled up and we couldn't get another forkful on. Then it was "Gee up Tidy. Gee up Tom." Off we would go into the field, climb onto the load, stick your fork in and then start to throw and spread it over the field.

Do that a time or two and it is then dinner time. In for dinner, muck all over you. You were allowed to wash your hands before you had your dinner when you had been muck-plugging. You would hear one of the women folk say: "Go steady with that bowl of water, it will have to do for the lot of you. The pump is running dry and we want to do a bit of washing."

However, it comes to your turn to wash. You dabble your hands in the liquid, finish them off on the, by now, soaking-wet towel, dash in, stick your legs under the table, gobble away at a basin of boiling hot broth, followed by boiled beef and veg, finished off with treacly dumpling on the same plate. Your stomach put everything in the right order when it got there and, by gum, it had a struggle sometimes.

It was the same job after dinner. You were allowed a drink and a bite at three o'clock when leading muck. A mug of tea and a piece of pie with mucky hands? "Huh! What won't fatten will fill. Get it down, it'll soon be supper time again." In those days the three daily meals were breakfast, dinner and supper. You went from six at night until six in the morning, so the third meal of the day was supper.

CHAPTER NINETEEN

The months passed. Ted had got his pub in Driffield and was now on the point of going. We were sorry he was going. His wife was a wonderful woman, one of those rare people who could bring up a family of ten and keep control of them all, have ten men "living in" and feeding us all well. She got a name on the Wolds as keeping one of the best "tables" in a long walk and always seemed to have a smile and a word for us all and she had had time to "mother" me when I had my accident.

She went to the Bay Horse where she and her daughters, some of them now teenagers and as bonny a gang as could be found anywhere, soon made many more friends and also customers. The Bay Horse prospered and, like prosperous pubs, in time had to be demolished and a spanking new place built. The old place was cleared and is now the forecourt, and the old barn with so many memories and its contents have gone also, but I still remember the old place with its three steps jutting on to the pavement, the smokeroom on the right, the bar on the left and a tiny snug down the passage. It is a lovely thing is the memory of suchlike.

We got a new foreman. He had been foreman on one or two small places, but Warren was his first time as foreman and hind on a big farm. He was full of big ideas as to how a farm that size should be run, and after Ted's easy going way of getting done on time without causing any friction, Black Jack's method, as we soon called him, didn't go down too well. But we were hired, and as hired men we had no say. Mr J. W., the boss, hardly ever interfered with the running of the farm, so what?

Black Jack kept a really good table, but then, so did Ted, but whereas Ted sent you off on your various jobs and left you to get on with it, Jack was chasing you across every field. As one of the lads put it: "He comes down the bloody hedgeside like a lamplighter."

Funny how your mind goes back to those old times when the Driffield streets were lighted up with gas lamps and Jimmy was the town lamplighter. He was a tall, thin chap, but whether he lit them at so much per lamp or had just so much time to do the job in, he was always in a rush as he went from lamp to lamp with his long pole with the oil light burning in the brass holder at the top.

Nostalgia! Those evenings in late Autumn, when we played in the street in the glow of the gaslamps. By seven o'clock the streets would be deserted. Everyone, particularly the young, would be amusing themselves in their own homes and not as now, gallivanting about the town as long as they wish. But of course in those days the town "Bobby," if he thought you were out too late, would tell you to "clear off home" and mean it. They commanded a lot of respect from us lads did the police of those days, and when you knew that over-stepping the mark meant the reformatory, it increased that respect.

Fish George, why he was called Fish George nobody knew, but everybody did know that he had the loudest voice in Driffield. He was the local paper "lad." What age he was nobody knew, but I remember my Dad remarking once that he was an old man when he was a lad. But on a clear night you could hear him shout out his papers at the north end as far as the waterworks in Spellowgate.

It was November 1918, and the first Hirings Day, November 11th, arrived. It was a recognised day off for all the lads to go to the Hirings, whether they were staying on at their present place or leaving it on Martinmas Day on the 23rd. So off I went with the rest of the lads to Driffield. But what a day to remember it turned out to be. The excitement when the official news of the armistice came through. Driffield Market Place had never seen such a rush and crush. The pubs were overflowing with people. There was dancing and singing in the street.

Hiring was forgotten by most, although I got myself hired to go to a farm at Arram and took the five shillings "fest," which I immediately spent. I well remember the farmer who hired me telling me that as the war was now over, all the lads would be coming home and it would not be long before jobs were scarce and wages would come tumbling down and that I was lucky to be sure of a good job for another year before it happened, but it was another two or three years before it happened.

Still, I was now seventeen and his talk went into one ear and out by the other. I had his five bob in my pocket and I wanted to be in the revelry. Eventually the day ended and we wandered our way back to our "spots" for another eleven days' work, then it would be pay day, then off to my new spot. But things just don't always work out like that.

The next day Black Jack came to me as we were ploughing and started talking as we went across the field. "Has thou got hired?" he asked me. "Yes," I replied, "I'm going to a small spot at Arram." "How much has thou got?" he asked, meaning how much money had I been offfered for the year. I told him £35 and a five bob fest. "Um," replied. "Thou knows old Charlie is retiring."

He was the beastman and had worked for J.W. and his father for many years, but now he was feeling both his age and his rheumatics and was going back to this native Norfolk where the winters were kinder, so he said, and as his sister had just been widowed she would look after him. "Yes," I said, "Why?" "Well, I thought you would like beastman's job. It's a change from looking after horses. Thou has got hired before leaving this spot, so all you have to do is send back the five bob fest you got from him telling him thou's staying on here and he can't do nowt about it. " "That's all right, I know about that, but I've spent the five bob. It was a big day in Driffield yesterday. Everybody was out either boozing or singing." "That's nowt," said Black Jack. "We can get over that. I'll give you a ten bob fest if we can come to some agreement." "Right," I said, "I will think it over."

I didn't really want to go to Arram. It was only a hamlet, but it had a railway station. All the same, my thoughts were turning to finding a job in Hull, so I thought that if I got the Winter over with some nice warm beasts to feed and two cows to milk, come Spring, if I could get engaged weekly instead of being hired I would pack farming up and try my luck in the town.

Two days later the foreman asked me again if I had decided. "Yes," I replied, "Fifteen shillings a week and my food." "All right," he said, "it's a lot of money and you will have to earn it, so you will come back after Martinmas week as beastman." Ever been had! Crumbs, what a let up!

Old Charlie had been a part of the farm or even the family. He had moved with them when they moved from a Holderness farm to the Wolds and had been a favourite of J.W.'s first wife and as such was privileged. He was one person whom the foreman could not push about; the other one was the shepherd who once told him to look after his bloody horses and leave him and his sheep alone! As you can gather they were not bosom pals.

It was shocking weather, with rain and snow, and the yards were full of beasts. I soon found out that I was getting no help with the stock, except for the usual loads of straw from the stacky which the horsemen brought each morning until it was light enough to start off for the fields. Charlie had never started work before breakfast. His milking was his first job after breakfast and the last before supper.

The turnips for the cattle had to be led from the field, three loads a day, and in the rain I found that I was taking longer to pull up the turnips, throw them into the cart and cut them up in the yard. I had a machine similar to a potato chip cutter which I stood in each tumbril in turn, then I drove the load of turnips alongside, lifted the handle, pulled a turnip out of the cart with a small double-toothed drag, bashed the metal part of the drag on the edge of the cutter, banged the handle down, and the turnip would drop through the bottom in slices — a laborious time-consuming job.

I was getting later each day finishing, so I started to milk the cows after we had had supper, but when the snow came in January, it was just too much, so I asked the foreman for help to fetch the turnips. I was told to get up earlier in the morning and milk before breakfast.

That did it. I had been feeding the beasts on white turnips which were soft and would cut in the crib cutter, but they were nearly finished and I would be starting on the swede turnips which were harder and would have to be cut by the conventional turnip cutter — a "thing," that is the best word for it. It had a hopper at the top which held sixty or seventy turnips which fell by gravity onto a barrel which had inch square cutting blades in a V-shaped pattern on opposite sides. These cut pieces an inch square and the length of the turnip when you turned a handle on one side which rotated the barrel and also a large balance wheel on the other side. The cut pieces dropped into a large scuttle placed underneath it.

Once you had done it for an hour or so, you wished the damn thing far enough. I also had to milk the cows morning and night at the weekends as there was no one else on the job who could or would do it. Of course, weekend milking or any work on the farm was a paid job. My fifteen shillings a week covered the whole seven days, and I could see myself stuck under the cows every weekend during the Summer. I thought I was being put on, so I gave a week's notice and I thanked my lucky stars that I had decided to go weekly instead of hiring last Martinmas. The gaffer J.W. gave me a good reference, so off I went; my destination the bright lights of Hull!

I got as far as Driffield, and there I met an old schoolmate. I hadn't seen him for a year or more, so we talked and I asked him where he was working these days. "Oh," he said, "I've left this district and I am working at one of those little dairy places just outside Hull. Does thou want a job? It's good money, a pound a week and your grub. All the milking is done before breakfast, but that's what you get paid for." "Right," I said, "where do I find out about a spot?" "Well, look in the 'Mail' tonight or each night and somebody will be advertising for a chap."

Sure enough in the same evening's paper there it was: "Wanted,

strong youth used to farm work. Must be able to milk. Apply ---
Beverley Parks area." So the following morning off I went on the bike to
investigate. It turned out to be a small place with two horses and about
fifteen cows, and the farmer had just been demobbed from the army. His
brother and father had been building the place up for him during the war
ready for his return, so I was the first workman he had engaged.

We agreed on a weekly wage of one pound and my food. I was to help to
milk morning and evening, help to deliver the milk on the round in Hull
during the morning, do the outside farm work in the afternoons, whilst
the boss looked after the feeding of the cows. "But," he said, "we have
just moved into the farm and the wife is not quite ready for you to come
to live in with us, so I have got a nice place for you to live in until we are
ready."

I didn't mind where I lived, so long as I got plenty of beef and pie for
breakfast and well fed the rest of the time, so I moved in and got it all.
They were an elderly couple and a bachelor son who had a small market
garden. There were scores right round Hull in those days, each one
sending a certain amount of garden produce twice a week into the town.
Some of them took their produce to an open market that used to be held
in Park Street and others had their own outlet at some of the green-
grocers in the town, who would pay just that little extra to get a regular
fresh supply.

The job went fine. I was now eighteen and enjoyed going each
morning delivering the milk, half a pint here, a pint next door. We had a
small milk can that held about three gallons which we kept filling up
from the large churns in the horse-drawn float. "Half pint, please."
"Yes, lady." Dab the measure in the milk, fill it, bring it up quickly, spill
a little out of it, pour it into the jug, dab the measure back again, get the
smallest possible drop in it, slap it into the jug. Do it quickly and the
lady would be so pleased to think she was getting a large half pint. Of
course with milk at tuppence a pint we all had to be careful.

Time went on. We had a good working system. We both milked in the
morning, then when we had finished I went for my breakfast and the
boss got the churns ready and measured, then went in for his breakfast
while I got the pony yoked up into the float ready for the off. Then one
day he said to me: "The wife has got your bedroom ready, will you move
in this weekend?" "Right." I didn't want to leave where I was, but he
wanted to save a few shillings on my board, so in I went on the Sunday
evening.

Monday morning I was up as usual at 5.30 a.m. and went straight to
the cowhouse. It was the usual procedure, finish milking, go in for
breakfast. The wife was sitting on a chair near the fire with a baby on
her knee. "Morning!" I sat down at the table, she put the baby down,
opened the oven door and brought the plate across to me and put it down.
It had on it one tiny rasher of bacon and a smear of dip. She pushed a
plate of bread towards me. All was done in silence. "Oh dear," thinks I,
"she doesn't like this set up." Neither did I! I had never had such a
fiddling piece of meat put in front of me. However, I gobbled it up, then
sat back.

She was still by the fireside. "Can I have a piece of pie please?" I
asked. She looked stunned. "Pie!" she said. "Pie for breakfast?" "Yes," I
replied. "I've always had pie for breakfast since I started eating."

"Well," she said, "this is where you finish having it, so there." When you are eighteen the only side you see is your own, so I got up from the chair in high dudgeon and went outside to get the float ready. Shortly afterwards, the boss came out from the house and remarked: "I hear you and the wife didn't get on too well this morning. She isn't used to farm work, you know. She used to work in an office and I've had quite a job getting her settled." "That's all right," I replied, "but I want some pie for breakfast." "All right, I'll see about some for tomorrow. I will be calling at my mother's today. She always has some for my Dad."

The following morning I went in for breakfast and as before was given a small piece of fried bacon on my plate, two slices of bread on another plate, while the wife sat near the fire. "Morning!" A weak "Good morning" was the reply. I sat down at the table, wolfed the bacon and bread, then looked up and asked: "Can I have a piece of pie please?" She stood up and opened a cupboard door and took out a saucer-size cheesecake, brought it to the table, cut it into four pieces, pushed one piece onto the bread plate and then burst out: "You and your blasted pie. I hate the whole blessed lot, the damn farm as well. I never wanted to come onto the place. He was just obstinate. Just because his family had always been in milk he had to. He said that I would get used to it, but I never will, and now a blessed lodger in the house. I'm sick of it!"

I ate my piece of pie in silence, then went out into the yard. The boss was there. "Did you get your pie, then?" "Yes," I replied, "and a lot more, but you will hear all about it shortly." He came out a bit later seemingly quite upset. "She seems right fed up doesn't she?" he remarked. "It seems as though you and her are not going to hit it off." "No," I replied, "I suppose there will have to be a parting and I expect it will be me" — the arrogance of youth! "Yes," he said, "I will have to try to get someone to 'live out' or someone from out of the village. It's a pity, we were getting on so well together." I worked the week out and then went on my journeys.

CHAPTER TWENTY

I went home with the intention of having a week or two's holiday, just as my father was being taken to the fever hospital with diphtheria, a nasty complaint in those days, so I told him I would get a job a little nearer and stay with my sister, who was younger than me, until he came out of hospital. So I scanned the "Mail" adverts again, and there it was: "Man wanted, able to milk and use a scythe."

I could do both, so off I went to a place just on the outskirts of Hull; a housing estate covers it now. It was two pounds ten shillings a week, live out, start at 7 a.m. and finish at 6 p.m. Nice short days, it seemed a gift of a job, with no Sunday work and alternate Saturday afternoons off.

The main turnover was manure. Turnover was the operative word. In those days — it was now 1921— there were scores of horse-drawn haulage firms ranging from one to twenty horses, plus the large railway stables. All were cleaned out each morning and all the manure thrown into the "muck hole" which in turn had to be cleared at intervals. That was where our man came into it.

At that time the big fertiliser firms had not got into action. The only fertiliser sold in bags was mainly from small local firms making it out of fish, offal, etc., and the fellmongers who sometimes used anything with their blood and bones, so we used to clear the stable yards of their heaps, take it to our yard, then fetch a load of wet or damaged straw off a nearby farm and gather loads of road sweepings from the corporation yards.

Only those who have seen it can talk about the condition of the streets in those days, when horses reigned supreme and left their evidence in every street every day. On a dry, warm, windy day your nostrils were full of it. Gangs of men and boys used to be out every day sweeping up and, of course, tarmacadam was not so freely used in the side streets, so the sweepings up contained large quantities of grit which all weighed heavy, so the whole lot was mixed and turned over and the hose pipe turned on and the whole lot allowed to rot. It didn't matter what it was. So long as it was animal or vegetable, it went in.

When we had got a couple of big heaps the Boss would have his day out to Selby on its Market Day, meet the potato growers and market gardeners and sell 60 to 80 tons of manure to be delivered in 10-ton lots to their nearest station. Then it was all hands to the muck fork and the hose pipe. The water would be turned on in the evening and would be spraying onto the heap until the next morning. Then we loaded the rullies and took it to the nearest railway goods yard, usually leaving a trail of water all the way; two or three loads of that in the wagon, then fetch a load of sweeping and a load from a stable to heap the whole lot up again, fill up the wagon from the heap, up to ten or twelve tons, and repeat the process until the yard was empty again.

Although able to milk, I hardly ever put hand to teat. One of the big sons used to do it. They only had three cows, and they were kept in the most squalid conditions. Until the end of the First World War, there were quite a few similar cowkeepers. The poor cows were never moved from their stalls except for the annual journey to the nearest place that kept a bull. Once that job was over, it was back home to the neck chain and the muck. We used to say that if they were turned out into a grass field they would starve to death: they wouldn't know what the grass was for.

Except for the odd change to get new blood, most of them had been born in the same stalls as their mothers had been born in. Knowing the conditions that some of the milking was done in and the hygiene used to store the evening milk overnight from the cow into the churn, when the churn was dumped into the water trough and the tap turned on to cool it off and left running for hours on end, it was most interesting to hear the excuses put forward when a sample of milk taken from the churn was found to contain added water. Of course the water always leaked into the churn; never had the water been added to the milk.

Time went on, then at last she arrived. I had heard about "our Marcie." She had been on war work in Leeds for two or three years and had been living in Leeds all the while and had not been home while I had been working for her father. But I gathered that our Marcie was some girl. About three years older than me, she was built on generous lines, a replica of her mother. During her stay in Leeds she had acquired a West Riding dialect which, to me, never seemed to be the same as the one we learned from our families whilst we were babies or quite young.

She soon started coming into the stable when I was having my packed lunch, particularly when George, her father, had gone to market. In some ways she was years older than me and in sexual matters she could be my grandmother, but we all learn, as I was to find out one lunch-time.

I had finished my sandwiches and was sitting on the cornbin top when she came in and walked past me, giving my knee a little nip as she passed, and then she lay down on a heap of straw, threw her arms behind her head and stretched out, showing a long stretch of bare leg. "Hey," I said, "you're showing your pants." "I certainly am not," she replied, "I'm not wearing any. Haven't you see a lass without any pants on before?" By now I was getting well roused up, but I wanted to play it cool.

I certainly didn't want to get too deep into the family. For one thing, I wasn't fussy about her mother. She was too bossy and Marcie looked liked growing that way too. I could see what would happen if we went too far and had to get married. "My goodness, a two pound a week labourer marrying my daughter! I'll give him hell, I will that." But I was still looking at that long bare leg. "Haven't you had a lass before?" she asked. "No," I replied, "Only nearly." "Come on then, lay down here and I'll make a man of you."

Yes, I thought, I don't mind being made a man but it's a daddy I don't want to be. But that dress seemed to have lifted a little higher and all my puritan thoughts were being submerged by my sexual ones. "What are you waiting for?" she said. "Come on." Sexual urges are stronger than any other. I dropped off the cornbin top and dropped down beside her. There was a quick fumbling of buttons on both sides and then the voice screeched across the yard: "Marcie, you are wanted on the 'phone. It's your boyfriend Tom from Leeds. Hurry up!"

"Blast," said Marcie. "He would spoil it." She jumped up and both of us knocked the straw off her back, all passion gone. Damn the 'phone, it bosses everybody. It rings during the night, you answer it in case it's something special and it's a wrong number. You go out during the evening and wonder who has rung. Dictatorially it rings, and be you high or be you low, harrassed to death or not, you pick it up to stop the blessed thing ringing and when you finish with it you either bang it down or gently put it down and say: "How nice to hear from them!" But boy was I glad afterwards that it had rung then — and besides there would be other chances, or so I reasoned!

I came into the yard during the afternoon for another load to find George, his wife, and Marcie and her brother in a deep confab at the back door. However, I got on with my job, and after a while I got a word with Marcie on her own. Strangely enough, our little "do" of the week before was never mentioned again between us. I asked her what was the matter, for I could tell there was something not right. "Milk Inspector's been round again sampling milk. He was only here last week and Dad didn't expect him for another month and he slipped a gallon of water into the churn. He will be for it this time." He sure was, and a week or two later when he paid me he told that he was selling his cows and that he and his son were going to carry on the business, so would I take a week's notice.

I had been spending most mornings during the Summer mowing grass where it was long in the parks. It was a sideline he had. We used to tie it up in sheets about four feet square and sell it to the various stables for the horses. It was the nearest most of them ever got to nature, because as soon as they couldn't do their work, they went to the fellmongers. They were no use back on the farm for work, so when I left the place George told me that I would be difficult to replace, but if I didn't get a job quickly he would pay me a shilling an hour during the Summer to mow grass for him.

Fancy, forty hours mowing grass for just two pounds, but then, you either worked or starved; there was no dole for farmworkers. As for Marcie I didn't see her for a few years until one day I was sitting in my van in one of the Hull streets when this woman passed with a pram and two small children walking beside her. She didn't notice me and I didn't let on, but it seemed to be the same brash Marcie, but starting to have that real belligerent, seedy look as though she had finished up with a two pounds ten shillings a week labourer — ah well, one never knows!

Right, thinks I, I'm sick of farming. I will get a job in town. I had developed a liking for the theatre, variety at the Tivoli and the Palace, but I think my favourite was the Grand theatre with its musical comedy, opera and plays. Drama never appealed to me, although I did occasionallly go to the Alexandra theatre which was given over to repertory at that time, because I remember so well being there when they were doing one of their melodramas where the heroine was a cripple and was limping about on crutches. When the wicked stepmother lifted her hand to strike her, a voice from the gallery shouted: "Hit her with your crutch, lassie." It really did bring the house down.

I had started to enjoy a glass of beer. It was cheap in those days, but everything is dear when you have no money or very little. The pictures troubled me not at all and never have done. However, when a farmworker stopped working so did his pay. There was no dole or allowances for them, so I had to be up early and try my luck at the various works, etc.

I started to go on to the docks, but an uncle of mine who did work on the docks told me I never would get started unless I knew one of the foremen, and the only place I would get to know him was in the pub or marry his daughter, a step I wasn't in favour of even if a foreman's daughter had fancied me, so I gave that up. But hard times were just starting and jobs were in very short supply. The slump was not far off, but we didn't know it, and what did not sink in was the fact that what goes up, in this case wages, must come down, and down they came.

In my hunts for jobs I started going to the Hull market place, where farmers gathered to sell their corn or do business with the merchants both in and outside the corn exchange. Quite frequently one could meet someone you knew in the farming community. They were great places to meet one another were the old corn markets.

Each town had its Market Day, when one or two pubs near to the Market Place had special licences to stay open all day for the benefit of the market users. Some of them took their little sample bags of corn into the smokeroom with them and did not move until the smack of palm on palm signified that a deal had been done. Be it a good deal or a bad one, no one ever reneged on it; the clasp of hand was a bond. There are no packed market places now. The farmer has lost a good excuse for a day out, not that it matters these days because he and his wife can jump into their car (or cars) and go anytime.

One afternoon I propped my back up to the wall and waited to see if anyone wanted either a cowhand or a horseman. The few pounds I had saved, twenty pounds, which seemed a lot in those days, had just about gone. I still had to pay for lodgings, and my desire for a job in Hull was evaporating, so I stood there and hoped, and then he came across: "Now, young man, are you looking for a job on a farm?" he asked. I said yes. "Can you milk?" he enquired. "I am looking for a beastman and someone to help on the land when required. I will give you twenty-two shillings a week and your food. But are you a dry-hand milker? I can't stand these wet-handed milkers, greasy, wet and messy."

I said that I couldn't agree more, so we struck a bargain. I was to start the following day. So off I went home to pack my bag and get my bike ready. There were no bus services to the villages outside Hull. The trams stopped at the city boundary, and what was then open country and fields of grass or corn is now the site of huge housing estates, each with its complement of those huge piles of bricks and concrete, the skyscraper flats. I have never lived in one or been in one, so I will pass no judgement on them, but they were a long way off in the future as I pedalled my bike on a fresh route to the west of Hull and liked what I saw.

The farmhouse stood in the centre of the village opposite the pond. It was the usual type with an ivy-covered front with a wall round and the foreman's cottage at the end, foldyard gates opening out to the main street and the pond. I went round to the back door and knocked. A fresh-faced, plumpish maid answered it. I told her who I was. "Come in," she said, "Mrs. P is expecting you."

So I walked into the large kitchen, which had an Aga cooker on one side, a large old-fashioned landsettle on the other alongside the big old fireplace, and a large scrubbed table evidently where the lads had their meals. I had seen much bigger tables, but I had never seen a cleaner. I passed a remark about it to the maid and won her over right away.

Chas, that was the name she was always known by, was a well-built lass a few years older than me, with that contented look on a very pleasant rosy face. Everybody liked Chas and most of the village lads yearned for her too. She was a good sport and always willing to have a bit of fun with us lads after we had finished work and were not going into the village. She would often come and talk to us as we sat round the fire in the kitchen. She loved a saucy joke, but if ever the session looked like getting out of hand, down would come the heavy hand, she would call us a "grubby lot of young devils" and clear off to her own room and lock the door!

I hadn't been in the kitchen five minutes when Mrs. P came in. She was a tall woman, well-spoken, 35-40, with that calm serene look that men like. She said hello to me and told me that her husband was out, but she hoped that I would settle down with the other lads and Chas would show me to our bedroom. So off we went up the back stairs to our room, the usual farm bedroom, containing three double beds with the lads' boxes each by his side of the bed. Chas said: "I think that will be your side." So I dumped my bag and then she said something I had never heard before. "And this is the bathroom, and you are allowed one hot bath each week."

Ye Gods, a bath every week on a farm. We who were the great unwashed part of the working populace, used to living and working on a farm where water was a special commodity that you bathed in until you started work, and then it was a bowl of tepid water shared with four or five others. Hands and faces were washed each morning, hands, face and neck each evening, and the clarity of the water when it came to your turn depended on your rank in the peck order.

I remember well one hot Sunday, myself and one of the other youngsters taking our things off and getting into one of the dew ponds in the pasture. It just happened to have quite a lot of water in. Oh dear, the foreman got to know. He shouted his head off: "You mucky little buggers. Don't you know that the hosses have to drink that. Why don't you wait for a rainy day to get a wash." Strangely enough we remembered it one evening during a thunderstorm. It was like heaven with the door shut.

However, back to my new spot. At supper I met my new workmates. It was not a big farm; there were six of us. The Boss, Mr. P, or as everybody knew him P.J., showed me my job on the farm, the cows and the rest of the beasts that I had to look after. Then he said: "Look across here. There is this lot coming up soon, sixteen young heifers all in calf, some of them calves themselves. Yes, they were a special lot I bought, well bred. I wanted to improve my herd, so I got this lot to do it. I got them fairly cheap and look what has happened. I turned them out into the Old Hall park and got a chap to keep an eye on them. He never bothered and it's three miles from here, so I didn't get there myself A blasted young bull from next field had broken part of the fence down and over the weeks has served every one of them. It's bad enough at their age, but it's a blooming scrub bull that old Nap (the farmer) ought to have had castrated a year ago, but he was too damn lazy."

However, as time went on they each bore a calf, most of them a good sized one, except for one poor little creature. Nature is very hard when it comes to the reproduction of species. So long as there is room in the body she will fill it, and this one, the smallest of the lot, tried to give birth to normal sized calf that was showing only one forefoot. Despite our efforts she was so small that we couldn't put an arm in to bring the other foot forward. To save her suffering any more the Boss fetched his gun.

One day as we sat in the kitchen having our meal, I thought, I know that face, so I asked: "Weren't you at the Grange three years ago when I was at Warren?" We had both thought the same thing, so of course we had a real old natter. He was two years older than me. He was always called Tommy. He was slightly deformed, and when I remarked about it he told me that it was caused through carrying corn from the machine on threshing days.

His Boss, Old Tommy, had told him to do it. He was seventeen at the time and not very big, but the old man was insistent that he must do it alongside one of the older men, so young Tommy had a go at it and managed. It was oats that they were threshing, and you could only get twelve stones into a bag, but the next week they were threshing barley which was carried at sixteen stones to the bag. When Tommy demurred he was told that it was only four stones more than the last lot and he managed then, "And besides, I'll give thou a going over if thou doesn't shut up and get on with the job."

That was a threat, and young lads like Tommy with no one to back him up had to do as they were told. Old Tommy had a poor reputation as a farmer and as a boss. The inevitable happened. Tommy didn't get the bag of corn laid correctly on his shoulders from the lifting barrow. He had very narrow shoulders, and he tried to carry it away, but of course it started to slide. Tommy hadn't the strength to hold it and down he went.

When he tried to get up he couldn't. They finally got him to bed, and after a few days rest he was able to get up but he couldn't straighten up properly. He was told it was just a bit of a strain and he would be all right in a week or two, but he wasn't, and Tommy became one of the many farm worker casualties who had carried corn too early before they were strong enough and for the rest of their lives suffered with back trouble and in many cases deformity.

Compensation? Not on your life! It was an occupational hazard. It had to be an accident resulting in permanent injury preventing you from working for some considerable time to get any money. It made me more determined that ever that I would never carry corn for anyone. Tommy was not with us long; he finally got a job in Hull that he could manage.

CHAPTER TWENTY-ONE

I got off on the wrong foot the first Sunday I was in the village with her Ladyship, the wife of Sir James who lived at the Hall. There was a low wall along the side of our farm facing the pond and near to the church, where the lads of the village had sat and gossiped for years. In fact the wall top was worn bright by the seats of corduroy trousers sliding on and off it. Lads had sat there waiting for their sweethearts or a chance encounter with one of the maids coming out of church and the pleasure of taking her for a walk back to the place where she worked. There would be a self-conscious "Cheerio lads," and if it was a fine evening, a gentle slide off the wall and wander off to the girl of his choice.

However, this first Sunday morning I was sitting with five or six other lads when suddenly they all slid off the wall, all caps off and in the left hand, the fingers of the right hand to the side of the forehead. Myself, I still sat on the wall top and watched an old lady seated in one of the old bathchairs, a page boy in front holding the long steering handle and a footman at the rear pushing.

As she passed there was a chorus of "Good morning, your Ladyship," and then when she had passed there was another chorus of "Why didn't you stand up? Your Boss will get a letter tomorrow telling him to speak to you about it. He is one of the tenants and they all have to kowtow to her." Sure enough, he told me on the Monday night that he had had a letter from her wanting to know why a certain young man had not shown due respect to her and would he please mention it to the young man concerned!

The wind of change was already beginning to blow through a lot of the villages by now. The young men were coming back to the land from the army with different views of authority, and some of the old gentry resented it, but they themselves were moving with the times. Very few coachmen were required now. Instead it was a chauffeur. The large houses with big gardens were getting motor mowers instead of the hand mower pulled by a pony led by a young garden boy.

Some of the huge greenhouses once full of peaches and nectarines had been neglected during the war and were not being repaired as the labour force was being cut to save expense. The indoor staff of girls were now refusing to get up at 5 a.m. on washdays and very often other days. They were still, in a way, slaves, with their long hours and their two halfdays a week off and the strict orders to be in before 10 p.m. or the door would be locked.

It was a good working place; we all got on well together. We had a young fellow working with us who was supposed to be learning farming. He had come just before the war finished when he was seventeen. His family was quite well-off and he was on "work for keep" in an effort to keep him out of the army. He was far from being an A1 recruit, but he was a real Londoner and he fitted in with us farm lads and the rest of the village also.

He was a Jew and as such came in for quite a bit of ribbing, but he took it all and came back at us with his own brand. He was the first Jew I had really met and I liked the sample. I haven't a clue to his full name, but I believe we called him Stanley and when we said cheerio to him as he left us for home he had the last sally: "I will always think of you when I pass a greengrocer's shop, you swede-gnawers with your cabbage broth." Never mind, we all liked him.

Our next new face was a big strong lad. Mrs. P.J.'s brother had been demobilised from the army and wanted to train for a farm manager's job for which he had to have a few years practical farming. So what other or better place than with your brother-in-law, and that was where Pete came in.

A ladies' man every inch of him, tall, with curly hair and blue eyes, he soon started to make his mark with the girls in the village and our Chas in particular, but his sister frowned on that; her family did not go running after maids and she did not want any complications there, so Pete had to try elsewhere for his fun.

But whenever he could get near enough to Chas it was a squeeze and a quick break away, but she was a lass that could warm any hot-blooded young chap up to search for bigger favours from her and that was Pete's consuming passion. It was a long, rambling farmhouse. At the back were the kitchen, pantries and outbuildings, and above them the lads' bedrooms and their bathroom with its own staircase from near the back door. Chas had a separate staircase to the maids' bedroom and the main staircase from the hall to the principal bedrooms.

Our bedroom window looked out to the main street but Chas's looked across the foldyard and was above the cowhouse. Whereas our bedroom window seemed to be hermetically sealed, Chas always had hers lifted three or four inches, a thing that Pete was quick to notice, so he set his lustful mind to work and came up with the idea that if he climbed to the top of the cowhouse he could just nicely reach the window and with just a little co-operation from within, he could manage very nicely thank you.

Come the evening, it was warm, there had been a slight shower, and Pete's loins were hot. Chas had gone to her room, so he got a ladder to get on the cowhouse roof and climbed up. But it doesn't matter what job you do, there always seems to be someone looking on. This time it was Bill the shepherd. He had just brought his dog into the barn and fastened it up and looked through the open top half of the barn door across the foldyard and saw Pete's performance.

Pete reached the roof ridge under the window, stood upright, and put one hand under the window to lift it up, but it was fastened, so he tapped on the window and Chas heard him and came to the window. "It's me," said Pete, "Be a good lass Chas, and let me in." Chas evidently thought nothing to the idea and brought the window down on his fingers, just gently, but it was enough to put him right off balance. Down he went, slid down the roof and then dropped onto the muck hill thrown out daily from the cowhouse.

Bill said: "I just gently walked away, but it was fun whilst it lasted." To Pete it was just another set-back, but he realised that he would get nowhere with Chas and he must have had a good excuse to give his sister about his messed up clothes. He finally got a farm manager's job and finished up as the agent on one of the large estates for the Earl of somewhere or other, a top job.

Bill, the shepherd and general handyman on the farm, was one of farming's misfits. Brought up in one of the orphanages, he had been sent out to work on a farm as soon as he was old enough. He was a slightly built man, short and with a stammer. He was a gentle sort of man; never a swearword crossed his lips. He had quite a good tenor voice and loved singing. Wireless was still a thing of the future, but Bill would have been in a seventh heaven with a wireless set and a book. He used to chide us younger lads about our language and boisterous behaviour, but we liked him. He was a good sort who couldn't harm anything or anyone.

We had in the village a couple who had retired from business in Hull and were now trying to organise the villagers into what they termed "constructional unity." Everyone was to do something for the village. It was a desperate piece of work to undertake, because most of the inhabitants of any village viewed with suspicion anyone who tried to do anything out of the ordinary. Usually those who tried it finished up disheartened and gave it up. However, this couple decided that they would have a concert in the schoolroom, and Bill was one of those asked to sing.

Bill needed very little encouragement to sing. His voice always rang out above all others at the Chapel, so he decided on his song and started to practice. Out in the fields all day he had plenty of chance to practice, and one day we were both working in the same field. I was slashing a hedge on one side, and Bill was ploughing and singing his song as he walked along. Just as he got to the hedgeside he reached the end of the first verse — "across the great divide." He paused, turned away from his horses, struck a dramatic pose, then on to the chorus "with someone like you, a pal good and true, I'd like to leave it all behind and go and find" — the horses turned and kept going along the headland, the plough trailing behind them.

Just then the Boss came over the hedge to me. "Look," he shouted, "look at that damned man! Look at those blasted horses, they'll break that plough, shout at him, stop them." But Bill hadn't finished his chorus. Both of us ran across the field to the gate. Bill got to his last line:

"We'll build a sweet little nest somewhere in the West and let the rest of the world go by."

He then turned round, stunned to find his horses gone. He ran to the gate. We all landed there together, but the horses were first. They had just turned out of the field, the plough still yoked to them. It had got wedged behind the gatepost. Crack went the gatepost just as we all shouted "Whoa" and the horses stopped. Poor old P.J. I thought he was going to have a heart attack; he suffered from angina. He shouted at Bill: "You blasted man, I promised my dear wife I wouldn't get excited over anything, but you have sorely tried me this morning."

The night of the concert came. It was a full house; the old schoolroom had not been so full for years. The MC announced: "Miss Jane will now sing for us." Jane started on too high a key, couldn't reach her high notes, which fell flat, and she was laughed off the platform. "For the next turn our friend Bill will now sing that well-known song 'With someone like you'." There were a few cheers and some hand-clapping, a few whistles and onto the platform stalked Bill and gazed at everyone through his extra thick glasses, gave a weak smile, then glanced at the pianist.

He cleared his throat and was about to burst into song when some "nutcase" at the back shouted: " Has thou tied thy hosses up, Bill?" The pianist stopped, so did Bill. The audience howled. His escapade in the field had become village gossip and was even in the nearby villages. The uproar died down, but not Bill. He thrust forward with a savagery no-one suspected he could adopt. "Yes," he shouted, "and if I had another piece of rope I would tie it round thy blasted neck just as tight."

We all cheered. Bill went up in everyone's estimation. He then turned to the pianist: "Right, Mary, let the battle begin." Of such are legends begun. The rest of the concert went off all right, except for the cobbler who was to give a recitation but forgot his lines halfway through and had to ask someone to get his copy out of his top coat pocket. Myself and Jim, one of the lads at the farm, gave a mouth-organ duet which was the last item on the programme. It literally nearly brought the house down, as one of the audience who had been sitting on the window sill got tangled up with the curtains and brought the whole blessed lot down — it was a red-letter night.

I had finished slashing the hedge in "Bill's" field and had moved into the next one with my slasher, a field that had a barley stack in one corner. It had been led there during the last harvest, which was quite a regular thing where the sheaves had a lot of bottom growth, that is, where clover seeds had been sown whilst the barley was quite young. Sometimes it was sown at the same time, and if you have a wet, warm Spring the clover would grow nearly as high as the barley, so that when the corn was cut by the binder, each sheaf contained a lot of green and clover at the bottom. If it was stacked before it was completely dry, it would heat in the stack, sometimes causing spontaneous combustion, and then you had a stack fire.

But this one had been there some months, and as it had not been thatched or much straw put on the top of it to turn off the Winter rains and snow, it was fairly wet well down into the centre of the stack. That plus the depredations of the rats and mice meant that it would soon be a worthless heap of straw. If a corn stack in a field was not protected by a wire net round it, a colony of rats over a few months would work their way from the bottom to the top making runs into the centre for their nests by biting the straw away, and their rate of breeding meant more mouths to feed every day. On the whole that stack was not much of an asset as a stack.

I was standing in the ditch cleaning the long grass from the hedge, and as I looked up I noticed the Boss walking across the field. He hadn't noticed me, or if he had, he didn't bother to come across. But that was not unusual, so I thought no more about it until about an hour later I looked across at the stack and one side was burning merrily.

"Gosh, a stack fire. Do something." It had always been drummed into us, if you see a stack on fire, if you can't put it out, get help quickly. I rushed across but there was nothing I could do. There was a ladder at the foot of the the stack but that was all. So off I went up the lane to the farm. The first person I saw was the Boss. "The barley stack down the lane is on fire," I shouted. "Oh, is it?" he replied, "it was all right the last time I saw it. We had better do something about it. Is it well alight?"

I knew that there was no phone in the house and that he would have to go to the village post office to ring up the fire brigade. "Aren't you going to ring for the fire brigade?" I asked. "Yes, I will get my bike out and go as quickly as I can." "Yes," I replied, "but the damn thing has been in the saddle house with flat tyres for weeks." "Ah yes, son, but in my condition I must not get myself harassed. I will pump the tyres up and go to the post office and ring the fire brigade. In the meantime you get a pitchfork and go down to the stack and see what you can save. It is a pity all the other men are at the other side of the farm; they won't know anything about it. I think I ought to go and get them to come and help you on my way to the phone. However, off you go." So off I went thinking on my way some folks are queer when it comes to a stack fire — I didn't realise it was me that was queer!

It is amazing how long a stack will burn without seemingly getting any less, and even when the fire brigade arrived an hour or so later there was still a goodly heap to burn. But, of course, as with all stack fires in the fields, as soon as they had used their supply of water, that was it. The outsides fell in, there was one huge flash and that was it, they could do no more. The insurance man came to see me one day a while after. I told him what I had done. "Oh yes," he said, "and your employer got his cycle and rode down to the phone." "Yes," I replied. "Oh, very good, good afternoon." I would say the insurance would be worth twice as much as the stack, but then, that was what farming was all about.

CHAPTER TWENTY-TWO

One warmish evening, I made across the yard to the saddle house and I heard a concertina. I remembered hearing it as a youngster in Aunt Jane's lodging house, but it couldn't be Old Corney — he seemed to be a hundred years old when I was a lad. But it was. He was one of the best known of the Wold Rangers. He and his concertina roamed the Wolds and the farms for years, always earning just enough for beer and tobacco and getting his food for work; a likeable type, a few squeezes on the box and the women would give him all the tea and sugar he wanted.

"Hello, Corny," I said, "you are a long way from your old patch." He didn't know me until I mentioned Driffield and the old place, then he fell about me: "Yes, I remember, my boy." So we talked and talked about some of the old regulars, about old Soldier Bob who bought his own rocking chair and allowed no one else to sit in it, and about Big Pete, who used to look after the place for Aunt Jane, and how he lost his arm in the Boer War so that his bit of pension and living free in the lodging house kept him going. He told me that at one period there were five Wold Rangers living there who had been in the Boer War as regualr soldiers. I asked him what he did now that he was getting older and how he had become a Wold Ranger, just as quizzy youngsters do talk to lonely people who want them to talk to them, and he told me his story.

He was born and worked on a farm in the West Country and courted and wed his Boss's daughter, but on their wedding night he had too much to drink. She didn't forgive him and refused any lovemaking or affection of any kind completely. She said she would look after the house and cook for him but that was all. Then one day, he told me, her Dad told him to go to town to fetch something, so he had better slip down to the cottage and tell her that he wouldn't be back for dinner.

"So off I went, and opened the back door. There was a grocer's travellers bike in the kitchen. All was quiet, then I heard the bed squeak in her room, it always squeaked when she got into bed. I heard her say: 'Come on,' so I gently locked the back door, took the key to her mother at the farm and walked right off the job with what I was wearing and just walked and finally finished up in East Yorkshire where I joined the East Yorks Regiment and did fifteen years with it as a single chap. When I came out I stayed up here and here I am. I stay in the workhouse in Winter, go out with my concertina and do a bit of work in Summer and my five bob pension keeps me going very nicely."

I said: "How about your wife?" "Oh her, I don't know. I haven't either asked or seen her since that day and that's forty years ago. I worked as a civilian on an army camp during the war, had a marvellous time." I was able to tell him what had happened to one or two of his old cronies, that Cottam Jack and Goudie Joe had joined the army and that most of them, same as himself, had been more or less forced into regular war work.

It was the 1914 war that finally put an end to the Wold Rangers, a body of men, mostly ex-soldiers (very rarely did one meet an ex-Navy man) who owed allegience to nobody, worked when they were forced to, never went hungry so long as they had a piece of copper wire to make a rabbit snare or "snickel," and the only goods they possessed they carried in a bag fastened round the waist with a can for boiling their tea and an enamel plate to put their eats on, particularly if it was a bit of roasted rabbit!

Corney stayed with us for only two nights. There was no work that he could do on the farm. Hard times were starting, and hard workers were finding jobs difficult to find. So off he went on his travels. His itinerary was to make for Market Weighton then along the top of the Wolds and finish at Driffield or Malton workhouse for the Winter. I watched him go down our village street, a bent and lonely man. He had made his own life, he had lived it as he wanted to, rightly or wrongly, but he went with his "ditty" bag and his concertina wrapped in a piece of oilcloth in a separate bag over his shoulder. I never saw him again, but those chaps never made old bones. One could cast a glance at any derelict person and wonder: "Is there a story behind that junk?"

It was Sunday and we were sitting in the saddle room. The previous owner of the farm must have kept a number of hunters and a groom. The large backyard had a number of horse-boxes and stalls for four horses joining the saddle room, which had a fireplace in it and steps to a room above it. We lads used it as our bothy. P.J. didn't keep any hunters. However, I was sitting there reading the paper when in walked Tommy. He had been left us about two months then. After the usual greetings and talk he said: "I am getting married next Saturday, will you be my best man?" I said: "You've left it a bit late." "Yes,"he replied, "but we never thought of it and her brothers are all too young, so we both thought of you." "Right, I'll go and ask Pete if he will milk for me next weekend."

The following Saturday saw me and another three of the village lads at the bride's village church. What a motley lot. The bride seemed to be related to everyone in the district, mostly by her older married sisters who had all brought their offspring. The wedding safely over we all adjourned to the village hall for tea and a party. What a party!

There was a pub next door and they fetched the beer in buckets and you just dipped your glass, cup, mug or what you had into them. It was a hot night and the buckets were kept filled. The singing and the dancing went on. I suddenly thought: "What's the time?" My train, the last train to stop at their station, was at 10 p.m. It was well turned that; there were no trains on Sundays, and I had promised Pete that I would be back during the Sunday afternoon.

Never mind, on with the motley. The bride's mother said: "We can put three of you on our sofa, but you won't be able to lay on it, it's a bit narrow." So after the party finished, off we went. The happy couple had gone, and we clumped into the front room, everybody feeling merry. It was a tiny room with a sofa and a table on one side and a partition down the middle. The bride's father shouted: "Don't make a lot of noise, there's others in there besides you."

We sat, we turned, we finally saw dawn break. Thank goodness, we can get outside and have a rest on the lawn even if there is dew on it. Breakfast started at 6 a.m. Dad and one of the lads had to go to work milking. We had started our breakfast when in walked Tommy. We stared: "I thought you had gone away," I remarked. "No," said Tommy, "we missed the train and we slept in the same room as you noisy crowd." "Good Lord," I said, "what a party! Fancy sharing your bride like that!" "Oh, it was nowt," remarked Tommy, "we started off a while back!"

Breakfast over, I set off for Brough. Someone had started a bus service to Hull, so they said. From there, gosh it was hot, the villages came and went, Staddlethorpe, Gilberdyke, Newport, North and South Cave, Elloughton, and finally Brough. Then I had a short ride on the bus, one of the early solid-tyred open-topped ones. Never mind, it got me within a mile of the farm, footsore and weary. The cows had to wait an hour or two extra for milking!

It was Saturday, payday; the Boss gave me my money. It was one pound two shillings per week and my food. "Look, Harry," he said. "I have been thinking. I can't pay you all this money any longer, so we have decided that Pete can look after the stock and that you can stay on, if you want to, for fourteen shillings a week. Take it or leave it." Times were getting bad. I had been trying for some time to get a job in Hull, but had certainly kept the idea to myself. What could I do, there was no dole for farmworkers and I had to live and I wanted a pair of new breeches and leggings.

The village tailor was recognised as being the best breeches maker for miles round. He and his son and two workers supplied landowners, farmers and farm lads with breeches of all qualities to suit all pockets, but they all had without exception his own particular cut, the seams coming down the side standing off a little above knee-height then making a sharp turn to the kneecap and finishing off with four buttons. With a pair of either leather or fustian leggings the farm lads looked as smart as his Lordship, sometimes more so.

Most, or should we say all, farm lads wore trousers and breeches made of corduroy with a calico lining for extra warmth, and the flap front was still the official make of trousers instead of the present zip or button fly. The two sides fastened in the middle with two buttons and the two side halves were fastened with two tapes, leaving quite a large gap which was covered by a large flap that hung down the front in undress, but when dressed you lifted it up and fastened it at the waist by buttons on the trousers. The pockets, on the two side flaps, were then covered.

They were warm to wear, but of all the fastenings, give me the old button ones: they never stuck. The old bell-bottomed trousers which at one time were the trademark of the farmworker were now just about obsolete, and the village tailor was having to fight hard for a living against the new High Street tailors with their made-to-measure suits selling at two pounds, and we young farmhands were starting to find a new life growing around us.

We had Saturday afternoons off and could now join the football and cricket teams or go into the towns to watch the big clubs play. Motor cycles were now coming on the market, but as yet were far too dear for us farm lads to buy. I had to wait a long time for mine, but it did come, as did a car, in their good time, but for the preseent I had my bicycle and could get about quite a lot on that.

One morning the Boss said to me: "I have bought four calves and a two-year-old filly at Ellerker. The calves are six months old, so I'll take you in the trap shortly and you can bring them back." "What!" I said, "Bring back four calves and lead a horse all that way? The blessed calves will be fresh and run all over the district!" "Oh no," he replied. "Mr. Allison's nephew will bring the filly, you will just have to look after the calves." Good, that satisfied me, so off we went and in due course arrived at Ellerker, and went to the farm in the centre of the village.

By this time the sun was full out and it was blazing hot, so we went into the yard. The filly was tied to a post and the beasts were loose in the yard. The Boss took me across to the young fellow who was to be my mate back to our place. As we were going across the yard he remarked: "I don't know if you know or not, but Harry who is mating you is blind and has been since he was a boy." Lummy, I thought, we are on something good today Harry boy.

By then we were with the other Harry and I met for the first time a man who was to become one of the best-known workers for the blind in the East Riding, Harry Allison. He became full-time organiser for the Blind Institute and travelled the East Riding organising whist drives, sales of work and any other fund-raising efforts. He travelled by bus and train, walking between the various villages. He had an uncanny sense of direction, and once he had been to a village he knew his way on his next visit.

He became well known on the bus routes and on the railway, and there was always someone to see he got off at the right stop. He did that for many years until he got a car and a chauffeur. He finally got married and went to live in Bridlington. We were good friends for many years, and it was a sad loss to the community when he died at quite a good age.

But back to our animals. The boss got back into the trap and set off home. He knew something did P.J.!

Harry's uncle helped me to get the calves out of the yard into the village street. There is a beck that runs through Ellerker, and the calves knew all about it. They made straight for it, and as we got one or two out, the others were back. We got hotter and hotter, and I was spending nearly as much time in the beck as they were, and I was getting wetter and wetter. Finally one or two villagers helped us to get the little brutes (by this time) onto the road for their new home.

Harry had been holding on to the filly all this time, quite unperturbed, so we shot off down the road to South Cave, down what is now the M62 motorway, and the calves were starting to feel the heat. They had stopped their galloping about and I was having to drive them now. Harry was quite content with his charge, and we were able to talk to one another. He had just returned from London where he had been training for his future life. I think he had been at St. Dunstan's.

However, down the road we went. The animals were wanting to stop or lie down on the roadside, and by now there were a few cars on the road. Not that that was any worry. Today that same road has traffic hurtling down it and at the end of it is that stupendous thing the Humber Bridge dominating the skyline, all within sixty years.

We got as far as Welton, but I knew there was a beck running through the village, and if the calves got into that we would lose the four of them because they would just drink and drink until they almost burst and then they would get colic and die. It would have cut quite a corner off our journey and a good distance of it would have been on a green road, but the risk was too big, so on the main road we went until we turned off for our place.

The last mile took us two hours. We arrived at the farm, one Harry as fresh as a daisy having led his filly every inch of the way, and the other Harry nearly on his knees, but still not as bad as those calves looked. Still, all animals are the same. We all had a drink, a feed and a rest, and a few hours later we could have set off for back.

CHAPTER TWENTY-THREE

I have always been a keen admirer of good ploughing, and even today with the present huge tractors and ploughs, the ploughmen who use them are just as enthusiastic on the whole as their forefathers were. But the atmosphere is not quite the same. Where once everything was quiet except for the few spoken words of command to the horses from their drivers and an occasional champ on the bit, we now have the drone of powerful diesel engines or the revving up as the ploughs drop into the soil. Then the shouting of the drivers, plus the diesel fumes, makes the follower of ploughing competitions a very special person. But then, in these days, thousands of people go and watch motor cars hurtle round a track until the air stinks with petrol fumes.

But back to "once upon a time." I had ridden my bike to North Cave to a ploughing match. The pairs of horses were arriving yoked to wagons bringing their ploughs, which were unloaded and taken up to their numbered pegs on the headland. Meantime the horses had their final grooming and their manes and tails were plaited up. There were two types of plaiting mainly used: the ordinary three plait and the rig plait, which took longer to do with the hair parted and twisted into two separate rows. The brass bells would be fastened on the top of the headband, the face brasses and martindales. After a final polish, the horse would be ready to be yoked to the plough.

Sometimes the pair of horses would be judged for the smartest turnout, sometimes not, but whatever the conditions the ploughman never took a pair of young horses. It was always his own pair, probably a pair that he had worked for years.

The horses were put to the plough, with traces that had been polished until they shone by putting them into a bag of wheat straw tied by each corner to the wheel of a wagon. Each turn of the wheel sent the chains turning and twisting all the way to the station or mill. One journey worked wonders with a set of traces.

The backbands were on, the traces fastened, the cobbletree and swingletrees were checked, the traces hooked on, and now the plough was set up to the correct width and depth of furrow. Is it nine inches wide and four deep, or is it eight wide and five deep? The stewards will tell him.

The ploughman has been told the number he has drawn when he arrived. Each competitor draws his starting point so he has had time to check what the land is like, but there is no walking across on his piece to plough. He views it from the ends only. There are no bookies shouting the odds, just a few quiet bets amongst the onlookers between themselves, because each man will be fancied.

The depth and width were set, the coulter clean and sharp, the slape clean and shiny, a good sock — one that has had a day's use, just to take the rough edges off it and make it shine. There must be no risk of any soil sticking to any part; it can leave a nasty scar on the face of the turned-up furrow and lose him points.

Jack and Jenny were finally yoked up, with the strings that the ploughman drives them with tied from bit to hand, one to nearside and one to offside. Jenny is his furrow horse; she has always been his furrow horse. It's stubble field, so all the ploughmen know what sort of a rig to make. A rig on stubble land is made by turning the first furrow to the right and coming back anti-clockwise throwing the next furrow away from it.

Right — our man gets his pair set straight, his eyes on his marker on the other side. The moment comes. "Gee up Jack, Jenny." He sets a small object such as a stone or anything sticking up in a direct line for his distant mark; not a sound except for a very quiet "Woave Jack" or gentle "Gee back, Jenny." His guiding strings will not be used. A good ploughman guided his horses by gentle commands: to go left was "woave," to go right was "gee back."

A few minutes later he is at the far side and looks back; perfect, straight as a die, not an inch out. He turns his pair round for to throw the second furrow out. "Woave Jack, woave Jenny" turns them anti-clockwise for this time only to face the return journey, and this is where he knows one slip or a small stone wedged between his coulter point and the plough sock could lose him points for tidiness.

He has to turn his next furrow away from the first one and his coulter point has to cut exactly on the line that it cut on the first run. The horse placings were now reversed. Jenny, used to being the furrow, was now on the land and Jack in the furrow. Jenny was well trained. She would be content to be there, but sometimes a "furrow" horse would be gently pushing its way back into the furrow, causing that little loss of concentration by the ploughman by his having to keep calling "gee back" to keep it in its right place.

Back to the starting point, the two furrows thrown out, perfect! Now to the second act, turning one of the thrown-out furrows back, plus a similar sized one from underneath. So, it's turn round again, Jenny back in the furrow, landwheel and furrow wheel to be adjusted again. They must be exactly right. "Gee up." Off again, turn round, right wheel this time, back to the starting point leaving behind a perfectly shaped and straight rig. The two double furrows are now set side by side and two empty furrows for the next turns to plough into. The judges have checked. He now only has to plough a stated number of turns, keep his furrow absolutely straight and he could be the winner.

Before the 1914/18 war competition was keen, and even between the wars to sell ploughs every district had its ploughmakers, but there were a few who before 1914 were becoming known beyond their own parishes, such as Saunders of North Cave and John Wood of Bilsdale who, in 1911, bought up a business in Driffield and started to make his ploughs there, mostly for the Wolds land.

I remember the first plough I ever used was a Bilsdale one. He made a variety of ploughs to suit the first and second year off lads, who lacked the weight and stength to handle the better and heavier ones which were real competition jobs. The firm is still in business in Westgate, Driffield, but they have moved with the times and now one sees huge tractors and ploughs that the original John Wood could hardly have imagined.

Yates of Malton were another maker of good ploughs and it was interesting to listen to discussions on the merits or otherwise of the various makes where farm workers gathered. But I think that the "Daddies" of them all were those produced by Ransome, Sims and Jefferies of Ipswich. They had been making ploughs from the early 1800's, and for a number of years had a team of Suffolk Punches and an expert ploughman to compete at all the large ploughing competitions and shows, advertising and displaying their selection of ploughs and other farm implements.

I think that they tried out a mtoor tractor plough in the early 1900's, but it didn't catch on. Probably it was too dear and labour and horses too cheap, but by the time there was a demand for them during the 1914/18 war, Henry Ford was producing his Fordson tractor, which was much lighter, and of course monopolised the market for many years.

Horse-drawn ploughs were still dominant until after the second war, but by 1948 very few horses were left on the land. Diesel and petrol took over from oats and chaff as the food for the power. There was no hiring, no tied men, and one of the songs the young ploughman used to sing no longer had any meaning; there was no need to run away, a week's notice was enough:

Once I was a jolly ploughboy ploughing in the fields all day
When a very sudden thought came across my mind and I thought I'd run away
So! Now it's hurrah for the scarlet and the blues
See our helmets glitter in the sun
As your bayonets flash like lightning
To the beat of a military drum
For there is a flag in dear old England
Proudly waving in the sky
And the watchword of our soldiers
Is, we will conquer or we will die.

Whilst I was hired at Warren I had made friends with a lad whose home was at South Cave. He was hired at Wold Farm next door, so one Sunday I thought I would have a ride over to South Cave and see if I could find anything of him; it was only a few miles off. He and another two lads had been hired to a farmer in the South Cave area who had taken the Wold Farm over at Lady Day and come with him. I remember we sent some ploughs over to give him a ploughing day. Most of his neighbours would send some. It was a usual thing to do to help any new tenant to catch up with his ploughing, as otherwise it could mean that he would be too late getting his land ready to sow his Spring corn.

However, back to South Cave. After asking a few folks I found that his father had a small market garden, one of dozens in that area, and it happened that when I got their my friend Ron was at home for the day. His mother invited me in for a meal and introduced me to her grandfather who had just come across to see her. He lived nearby with his daughter. As soon as he heard that I was a Woldsman from Driffield he started to tell me about himself.

He had, as a young man, lived at Garton, a village near to Driffield, and when I mentioned an uncle of mine who still lived there, my grandmother's oldest brother, he said: "What, Bob Marshall? I worked with him seventy years ago (that would be about 1850). My father was a pond-maker, and Bob worked with us until the business closed down." Most farms by then had got a pond and there was only the odd dewpond to be made.

He then went on to tell me that it was a Driffield man in the late 1700's who invented a way to make ponds on farms, particularly on the chalky land, that would hold water. As he said, anyone can make a hole in any sort of land, but making it hold water during the Summer is another thing altogether. The old chap had got a listener, so off he went with his talking about pond-making.

"Yes," he said, "we had a gang of about ten men, sometimes less if they were a bit quiet on the farm and the farmer wanted to use some of his own workers, and in bad weather he could have ten men kicking their heels, so he would certainly not want to pay for exta labour. The site of the pond would be fixed as near to the stables and foldyard as possible. He might want a pump in the foldyard to draw water to fill a trough or tank for the cattle or horses or a high pump on the edge of the pond so that they could fill the water cart in Summer to take down to the fields for drinking, so the depth and lay of the pond could be fixed.

"Then the digger would start. Not those huge monsters that take a ton of earth at a time as we have these days, but those men who pushed a spade into the ground, lifted one spadeful, and threw it into a cart. There would be three diggers to a cart, and half a cubic yard to a cart load, but when one was digging from six a.m. to six p.m. and no lazy minute, a small hole soon became a large one. The hole finished five feet deep at its deepest point near to the pump, the sides sloping down correctly. If it was too steep, the horses would jib at walking down the slope. If it was too shallow some of them would walk in too far if they were not held by halter ropes.

"Lucky were the diggers if they were digging clay out, their job was halved, but if it was on one of the Wold farms and they were taking nothing but chalk out the job was doubled. A hole in a bed of chalk and water runs out as fast as it is put in, so the first lining was put in. This was a mixture of clay and lime puddled well in, then a layer of small chalk was put on the top, then more clay and straw. If possible, it was as well to get a flock of sheep to puddle it in. They made the best job with their small hooves. They pushed the straw well in and made a really solid job of it. After that, a three inch mixture of small stone, gravel and small chalk, with a little soil to bind it, was made into a slurry and poured on the top. The gang had to ram it solid until the whole lot was as hard as the highway. All that was then left was for the rains and heavy dews to fill it.

We really had a good talk and after tea I got on my bike and went back to the farm. I saw my friend in Hull one Saturday night. We were both going to the Tivoli theatre. I said to him: "Tell your grandad that my uncle Bob died a fortnight ago. He was 96." "Well," he replied, "Grandad died a month ago."

CHAPTER TWENTY-FOUR

The tractor that had burst on us at Warren during the war period had not fired the enthusiasm of farmers in general, and the slump was now starting to bite. Money was getting scarce and a horse could replace itself, or at least a mare could, and its feed was produced on the farm. But there was one thing that was now becoming popular, and it was the motorcycle, the Douglas in particular, which reminds me of one of the first of the "left on the roadside" victims.

I had gone for a walk down the lane when I met her. She was sitting on the roadside crying. I asked her what was the matter and she poured it all out. A young fellow she knew had offered her a pillion ride on his new bike and she thought how wonderful it was until they got miles from home then he had stopped for a rest. They sat down on the grass, then he put his proposition: "You give in to me or you walk home!"

She decided to walk home and she was footsore when I met her and had another three miles to go at least, and she hadn't even got a penny for a tram when she reached them. I offered to go back to the farm for my bike and ride her "cross-bar" to the terminus. However, after a tearful outburst about never trusting a man again she decided that she would have to trust another one or walk!

So she gave in this time, but she kept her honour. I was soon back with the bike and she was of slight build so she got on the cross-bar and off we went. It was nothing unusual in those days. I took her to the tram, and when we got there I gave her the few coppers to get her home. She promised to let me have them back, but strangely enough neither of us had asked where the other lived, so my few coppers are still outstanding. I never saw her again.

Threshing days were still the same but now I didn't have to carry the chaff, and I stubbornly refused to carry the corn, so my job was always on the strawstack, which was the next worst job. As I wouldn't carry the corn I was not asked to deliver it to the flour mills in Hull. Most farmers within eight miles of the mills used to deliver to them. There would be two horses yoked to a pole wagon, and off you would go to the mill.

There the sampler took a sample from every load. If he had got a poor sample from a load he would be discussing it with the foreman and one of the buyers, holding everyone up. It didn't worry me about not going. Let Jack go.

What none of us did like was winnowing of the corn before it was bagged in the granary, turning that big handle that rotated the fans that blew all the light corn and bits out as the corn dropped by gravity from the hopper that had to be kept filled on the top of it, into bags hung from it. Damned old thing. Even my Uncle Kerry had a horse-driven one years before.

Another piece of machinery that tested your strength and your patience was the turnip-cutter. It was another heavy-framed thing with an oblong container on the top of it which would hold quite a lot of turnips. You put your scuttle inbetween the four legs underneath the cutter, got hold of the handle and turned the wheel like mad. If you turned it slowly you had to be one of those big chaps who could make any heavy job look easy. As you turned the handle it revolved a hollow drum which had sharp-cutting teeth, inch square holes in a Vformation, and as the turnips fell on to it, it cut them into neat pieces similar to our chipped potatoes.

Whilst you are reading this, let your mind gently drift into a sheepfold in the depth of Winter on one of the Wolds farms. It had been raining all the previous day, but the shepherd and his man, or men, depending on the number of sheep, have been pulling and cleaning the turnips and throwing them into neat piles ready for the next day's cutting for the sheep. Wet through, the two or three of them go home for their supper and to dry out.

The next day it's back to the sheepfold. The pouring rain has stopped and it is now sleeting, but daylight's breaking. The first job is to feed the sheep. The turnip-cutter is pulled up to the first heap of turnips, across the mud and slush. It has two iron wheels at the back of it so that most of the weight of it is on the puller. Then they start the cutting: one turns the handle, one forks the turnips into the holder, and if there are only two of them, he also empties the scuttle as it fills into the troughs for the hungry sheep.

Two hours of that and by now it is gently snowing, big fat flakes, as shepherd says, like pancakes. The sheep have to be moved forward each day to keep on the edge of the new heaps of turnips, four or five yards each time. The nets have to be taken up from behind to the front, the net stakes to be driven in for the nets to be fastened to.

Dinnertime; off they go. The bags they had had over their shoulders are soaked through, and their overcoats as well. Any bad weather clothing such as oilskin coats and leggings had to be bought by themselves and they were not cheap even then, for the farmer could never afford them. After dinner, back they would go to the fold, for there were turnips to be cut and clean for the next day and sheep to move into the new fold. One or two of them have got bogged down in the mud and so have to be dragged across and have some of the mud scraped off the fleece. At three o'clock it's time for feeding up again. A couple of hours later it's dark. There are a few inches of snow and a bit of wind getting up; there will be drifts in the morning. "Come on lads, let's get home." You didn't see many old shepherds on those hilltops. One thing I never wanted to be was a shepherd!

Old Drover Bob was a well-known figure in the village. He was getting on in years, but still did a bit of local droving into Hull cattle market to earn a few shillings towards his keep. He had made a home with a family of his own type and they all lived together in one of the cottages. He did little jobs at our place and of course we used to chat together. He had once been a Wold Ranger. Strangely enough, I found that most of the old Rangers were as proud of the title "Wold Ranger" as any of them had been of their old regiment, those that had been in the army.

I remember Bob telling me that he stayed at the little lodging house in Driffield and had roamed the Wolds for years. We got talking about the old pub and Uncle Kerry, and I told him about the old horse wheel at the back of the bar. "Yes," he said, "I remember that thing. There was a lot of them on the farms when I was a lad. The big threshing machines hadn't started travelling from farm to farm and the old portable steam engines were only on some of the bigger Wolds farms, but lots of places had the horse wheel. Some of them took two or three horses to work them. They were high geared so as to work a good-sized threshing machine and winnower at the same time.

"I also remember," he said, "some of the farms having a different wheel. It was a slatted wheel about two feet wide and partly let into the ground with just a certain amount showing above a staging where a horse wearing a collar was yoked to two posts by a short chain to each side of the collar and a heavy piece of wood dropped behind it which stopped the horse from backing out. The locking bolt was removed, the horse started to walk, thus turning the wheel and the shaft drive into the barn."

Old Bob thought they were more efficient than the turret and shaft-driven ones. Heavy horses were no use on the slatted wheel. They tired too quicky. The best horse was either a heavy pony or what was called a half-legged one, that is, a foal from a Clydesdale mare and a hunter stallion. Many farms had one or two. They were very useful for a quick trip in one of the light carts with a small load to market when you could break them into a trot without distressing them. Or a pair of them would be yoked to a light roller or a set of light harrows, and a young lad driving them could roll or harrow thirty acres in a day.

A year or two after I left the village I asked one of the lads if old Bob was still on the go. "No," he said. "The old lad got in the way of some bullocks in the cattle market and they knocked him down and I think he got trampled on. However, he went into hospital and didn't come back again." Poor old Bob, it would be a lonely finish for him.

I sometimes wander into our local cattle market on Market Day and muse on the quiet efficiency with which the whole job is run and compare it with the seemingly chaotic conditions of sixty years ago, when beasts were rushed into the pens from the railway sidings where they had been shunted. Poor scared creatures that had spent all their lives never hearing anything louder than the hum of the threshing machine were now rushed and slashed by the drovers hurrying against each other to get back to bring another herd in for the same treatment. Their tails were twisted and screwed and their legs kicked.

Sheep got similar treatment. They were jabbed with the end of stocks, had their legs grabbed and were pulled bodily into pens. Pigs fared no better, but stick marks showed on them, so their ears suffered instead.

Cattle markets of those days, with their muck and noise and violence on a wet day when tempers got very short, were shocking compared with today's markets. Now the animals come straight from the farm in a large transport nearly into their pens, or there is a small consignment in a trailer behind the farmer's car. There is no screaming and jabbing. The farmer thinks as much about his stock as does the R.S.P.C.A. inspector who is usually in the market casting his eyes on all and sundry handling stock.

Even those animals that have to go for slaughter are collected by transports and taken straight to the abattoir to be dealt with humanely, as against the old method, when they were driven to the slaughterhouse, which could be any old building. The slaughterman would be dressed in dirty overalls and a large leather apron ready with his poleaxe and knife to give the final blow, not always a first time blow either. If the beast was struggling in the slaughter pen, even a slaughterman and a heavy poleaxe took some handling to hit the exact square inch on the beast's forehead. Thank goodness for the tightening up in the slaughter-house laws and the invention of the humane killer, plus the building of new abattoirs, where sanitation and humanity are now an ideal and not a nuisance.

"Any chance of another shilling a week?" I asked the boss. "I'm getting that I can't manage on fourteen shillings a week. I am always broke and I want new working boots and trousers. Don't you think you could spare another 'bob'?" "No," was the abrupt reply. "I am just as skint as you are and I don't get fourteen bob a week to do as I like with, and besides you are not hired. A week's notice is all I want and you can go."

Not very cheering! I liked the spot and the village and I knew that if I left I would have to find another place quickly, and as it was not quite Spring yet I may have to wait quite some time before I found a fresh place. In between time I had to live, and in those days there was no "dole" or any assistance at all for farmworkers. Out of work in those days meant out of work, out of money, and if you were married could mean out of a house also.

I liked farm work. The hours were now quite good, 7 a.m. to 5.30 p.m., a real change from the old system of 4.30 a.m. to 7.30 p.m. in Summer time, a matter of fifteen hours a day. Of course, Winter hours were not so long, two hours a day shorter, but the horseman and the beastman had to feed up on Sundays, which meant another three hours, except for the poor old beastman, who also had to milk his cows twice a day. I liked my new-found freedom of the weekends. It meant that I could now play football on Saturday afternoons, and if I wished to I could go to see the professional teams playing rugby, which I liked.

That reminds me of one trip I made to Leeds to see a cup final. A party of us met at the station after having a few drinks. I was never a heavy drinker, I had seen enough of it as a child. We rushed to the train as it was just about to set off. We scrambled into a carriage, ten sitting, two standing, all men, and by the time we reached Selby, nature was calling very strongly.

By a stroke of luck we stopped right opposite a toilet. There was a rush for it and I was the last out, and before my turn came the whistle blew and as we made a dash back to our carriage I spotted a beer bottle laid on the platform side. I grabbed it joyously. "Saved," I thought as I jumped into the compartment and slammed the door. I turned round triumphantly to look straight into the eyes of the person who had taken my seat, a woman; oh, the frustation! And the next stop was Leeds!

We crawled there at about a mile an hour, or so it seemed. We finally arrived and I made a dash. It was a lovely new suit I had on for the first time, made by Fred Hornby of Driffield, and when Fred put a button on he put it on to stay, and could I undo that button? Could I heck!

I tugged and twisted at it, but there was no give at all. Ah, one thing, cut the damn thing off. Out with my pocket knife, stand in the stall — there had been one or two queer glances my way during the past few minutes. Never mind, knife at the ready. Slice, cut it off, and I slashed my blessed finger. Blood dropped into the trough below, to the cry from the man next to me — eeh, blamed lad cutting his bod off! Then Mother Nature stepped in. She had been frustrated so long she refused to relax and I was stuck there another half hour waiting for the moment.

CHAPTER TWENTY-FIVE

She was one of the nicest girls I have ever met, tall and slim. We hit it off from the first time we met at one of the weekly "hops" that we used to have in the wooden hut that was termed the village hall. Indeed, it was something to be proud of, because very few villages had any place at all except the schools for any sort of relaxation. It had been a W.D. hut at one of the local camps and had been bought for the villge by his Lordship, but I digress.

Her name was Amy and her father worked in the gardens at the Hall and we got on together very well. It was a lovely evening and Amy and I walked down the lane and then we sat down in the long grass — you could sit on the roadside in those days. We talked as young folks have talked since time began. A quiet moment, and my thoughts began to wander; so did my hand, but it was held firmly by a small warm hand. "No, my dear," she said, "if we do anything like that you know what can happen, and if it did, what could you do on fourteen shillings a week? Besides, my Dad would go mad and probably kick me out. Why don't you give up farm work and try to get a job with a decent wage, then we could think about getting engaged, but with farm wages as they are, and my Dad is the same as a farm labourer, it's a problem making ends meet, so you had better try to sort things out."

It was just the impulse I required. I had been thinking for a while that if I didn't soon make a move I was going to be a farmhand all my life. For one thing, I could never earn or save enough money to start a farm of my own on fourteen shillings a week and my food. I did think of trying to get a gardener's job at one of the private houses, of which there were many in the district, but even there the wages were poor and hours tying during the Summer, when there was watering to be done in the greenhouses etc. Of course, no overtime was paid, and as an unskilled man I would definitely be the dogsbody for all and sundry.

There was a new industry growing up in the land, the making of motor cars, and a lot of the gentry were now buying them and there was now a demand for chauffeurs to drive them. I thought that would be a good thing to have a go at, so I had a talk to his Lordship's man. He had been taught to drive at the works in Hull and he was an engineer by trade, so when the Rolls Royce arrived he was moved lock, stock and wife to a cottage in the village. It's strange isn't it what you can learn when you get talking to people in a casual way. It turned out that his father was my mother's cousin and I knew his parents fairly well and had visited them a few times as a boy, but as he was a few years older than me we had never met.

He told me that he was lucky that he was paid by the firm, so he had a good wage and the use of the firm's garage and workshop in Hull. If he went out in the evening to a dinner driving the Boss, he had only to tell the time clerk and it was added to his time sheet. "But," he said, "there are very few jobs like this. There are quite a few people round here who will pay for you to be taught to drive, but you will more than likely finish up with a family where the master wants to be driven into town in an immaculate car at 9.30 a.m. then collected again any time between 5 and 6 p.m. for return.

"In between Mistress wants to go shopping and you are stuck outside the shops and cafés for two to three hours in your uniform and wearing a hat that doesn't fit because it belonged to the last chauffeur. You get home, have your tea, get your feet up and there is a knock at the door. The family are going out to a dinner party, will you please have the car at the front door at 7 p.m. Turns out to be a filthy night. When you return at 11 p.m. you see them into the house where the parlour maid takes over, then drive round to the garage at the back of the house, get the hosepipe fixed up, a quick swill down, washleather off. The boss would have a fit if the car was not polished the next morning. Off to your cottage, it's now midnight. Never mind, you are going to a warm bed and the wife is already in it!"

Of course it was just the same before the war, when there were few cars, and before that when gentlemen kept horses and had a coachman and not cars but working hours and conditions were infinitely worse. Same call, same weather, except that the vehicle would be a coach. You, the driver, had yoked up the one or two horses depending how far you were going, put the warm blankets and hot water bottles or hot stones inside the coach. Everything had to be comfortable for the family.

You drive round to the side door, and you would then tuck them in, wrap rugs round them to keep them as snug as possible. Not a word would be spoken. You then shut the door, climbed into the driver's seat, wrapped a rug around your legs, pulled the waterproof sheet across you, turned up your coat collar, pulled your top hat tightly down on your head in case it blew off, and stared into the dark wet night. There wasn't much to see; your one candlepower side-lights are flickering, but they are good lamps, the candles won't blow out. With a shake of the reins and a quiet word you are off.

An hour or so later you are there. The footman comes out and opens the door as you stand by your horses. You are told to take them round to the stables. The host's groom will be there. You will unyoke the horses and commiserate with each other about the weather. He may have had to fetch one of the family from her house and will have to take her back after the party.

You join the rest of the visting coachmen in the kitchen and have a cup or glass of something — they varied a lot in hospitality — until the call came: Mr. Lloyd-Smythe requires his coach in ten minutes. Then you move quickly and repeat everything in reverse until you get home. Then you climb down from the driving seat, so stiff and cold your legs will hardly bend, open the door, after ringing the house door-bell for one of the staff to open it and greet the family back into a warm lounge and give them a hot drink before bed.

You? Well you haven't quite finished. There are the horses to stable and to rub down with straw wisps to dry them off. You then give them a feed, give the coach a wipe down if it is wanted early the next morning, then off to your cot for the rest of the night.

You could always tell which were the old coachmen in the village pub. They had deep wrinkles down the side of their jaws, and furrowed brows. They rarely smiled. Those cold winds and snowy drives seemed to have set their faces like granite, and when they stood up, their joints creaked with rheumatism. How do I know? Mother's brother, Uncle George, was a coachman for a number of years and I remember well the stories he used to tell me 60 years ago about life "downstairs."

He told me about the unbelievable hours worked by some of the indoor staff and the living conditions of the lowest grade, the scullery and kitchen maids, which were often made worse by one of their own, the housekeeper, who was often getting on in years and trying to justify her job.

And of course there were many places where meanness was carried to excess. One Mistress came through the back door one day (a good mistress never used the back door) and went straight through to the kitchen and announced: "I say, Cook, I have just been having a look round the back and I noticed the men have been limewashing the outhouses, and I also noticed that there was toilet paper in the staff lavatory. I think that is unnecessary. Newspaper is quite good enough for the working class — please have it attended to."

He told me about his last place before he left service for good. "It was a good place. We had a flat above the stables. Master was a bachelor, kept a good table, and an open house. He was a good rider to hounds, but he did a lot of visiting himself, and his trouble was he couldn't carry his liquor very well and would change from an easy-going chap to a belligerent bully, and of course the poor old groom got it."

He had been an amateur boxing champion at his university, and when the fit took him Uncle George had to go three rounds with him. Uncle George was a big fellow, well able to look after himself in any company, but as he said: "One night the master got a bit too rough with me. I had been up all the previous night with a mare that was having her first foal and I felt like having a scrap with anybody, same as he did, so I hit him hard, bloody hard. I carried him into the house, laid him on his bed, called the housekeeper and told her what had happened. I knew it would be the sack, but there are limits, and the following morning I was called to his study."

" 'Well, Train,' he said, 'it was inexcusable what you did last night. Why did you do it?' I told him. 'Well,' he replied, 'I cannot condone any violence on me from a member of the staff, so you will have to take a week's notice and oh, by the way, you are the only man who has ever knocked me out and I will help you to get another job.'

"I decided that I had enough of service and would like to try and get a job in the town, so I told him during the following week what I would like to do. 'Right-oh, Train, leave it to me.' He came across the courtyard as we were moving out of the flat and gave me a letter. 'Take this to Brown's office next week and they will fix you up.' I thanked him. He then put a half sovereign in my hand and said: 'To the only man who ever knocked me out, but don't boast about it'."

Uncle George said to me: "I kept that half sovereign until I had enough money to buy a gold watch and chain, then I had it mounted on the chain and look, it's still there." And so it was thirty years later and Uncle George still at the same firm. That put all thoughts of trying private service out of my mind.

So on the Saturday afternoon off I went to Hull to call on my sister and her husband, who worked in Hull, to ask him if he knew of any jobs going. He told me: "Yes, I was talking to Wilkie, the carting agent, this morning and he asked me if I knew of a good chap used to horses who wanted a job and I told him about you, so if you want the job get off to his house now." I was on my bike within minutes and down to Wilkie's place. "Yes, I was used to horses and I liked driving them."

He told me that all his drivers had been farm workers before they started with him so that I wouldn't be an odd man out and that he paid all his men the same, fifty shillings a week and you started work at seven each morning. If you were later than half past, your job was gone because there was always someone waiting for your job. I soon found out that this was true. Quick mental arithmetic told me that with twenty-two shillings a week lodging money to pay it would leave me twenty-eight to do as I liked with, and besides I was getting a foot in Hull and could look for a better job in the meantime.

I went back to the farm to give a week's notice to P.J. He was not too pleased, with haytime and harvest coming up very soon. All the best men were leaving the farms. No, he couldn't pay any more; he was sure that he would be able to replace me. Whether he could or not didn't bother me, I was going.

Down the village I went to tell Amy, and she had a surprise for me. Her father had given a week's notice at the Hall and was leaving at the weekend. He had got a better job near Goole, and as it was a tied cottage they would be going next weekend themselves. Consternation, we would be at opposite sides of the county, but we were sure that love would find a way. Ha, ha, so much for love. We each went to our different jobs. I found the fleshpots of town very alluring and we never saw each other again. Such is life when you are young. But some lad would get a smashing wife. She was lovely. I hope she did well.

From 1914 as a part-timer to full-time in 1915 at six shillings a week, expected to feed myself. Hired at Martinmas 1915 for £6 10s. for the year, and now it was 1922 and six different farms later. I was earning a maximum of £2 weekly and my food, starting work at 5.30 a.m. to get my ten cows milked by hand ready for delivery in Hull at one particular place. I was leaving farm work for good and I didn't think for one moment that I would miss that fourteen shillings a week and my food. Fifty shillings a week was a lot of money in those days.

What now? Seventy years on from my first starting on the farm. I am no longer the country bumpkin, the cartoonist's bread and butter, but a highly skilled person earning a wage that stands comparison with his like in the towns. I work a twenty thousand pound machine with the same pride as my grandfather did a pair of horses and his Bilsdale plough.

In those past days the larger towns such as Hull provided a source of young cheap labour at the yearly hirings, where many young lads wanting to go into the country stood at the hirings and were taken on very often by farmers who had just one or two lads and could only afford a further five pounds for another. But the lad got into farming life and after probably a rough, tough year of near slavery he would change places, settle down and become a first -class hand.

Not now. Jobs on farms are keenly competed for by lads in the villages now that larger schools in the country towns teach tractor work and servicing as part of pupil training. The lad who takes an interest in mechanical things has a head start on his competitors for the few farm jobs. Many times after I have given a talk on my reminiscences at various places I have been asked the question: "If you could return as a boy again would go you farming again?" and my answer is: "To go back to those days of near slavery, taking into account that a lad of those days expected all the discomfort that farm life as an employee gave him and the wages that just kept him or his family above the starvation point (there were only a few labourers who got free milk or even the smallest of extras) I don't think I would. But to go back to the present set-up with a legal fixed wage, security of employment, and where the farmer asks you to do overtime and every hour is paid for at a fixed rate, and where a lad can play cricket or football for a team without the fear of the boss telling that he can't go this afternoon or if he injures himself, he needn't bother to come back and he will get another chap to do his job who doesn't play football, I would say 'yes please'."

There would be quite a few differences that I would find. Firstly, instead of there being 15 or 16 of us at Warren, there would be two of us. Instead of 16 horses there would be huge tractors, and where that first Fordson tractor would only pull the implements that three horses pulled, these monsters rating over 240 h.p. with four-wheel drive have no limit to the work they can do. But the driver, a man now earning a good weekly wage, sits there. Whatever the weather may be, it means nothing to him. He is comfortable and with his ear-muffs or ear-plugs fitted, he is in a world of his own.

The one thing that I would miss most in this modern world would be the most simple and happiest of any occupations, walking behind the plough pulled by two good horses and singing at the top of my voice one of the old country songs, probably:

Only one more bag of the golden treasure
Said the gallant sailor as he kissed his fond young wife
Only one more bag of the golden treasure
Then we will settle down for life.
Yes, we will leave this shack for a little cottage
And enjoy the wealth we have earned
So she sent him forth with a lover's blessing
On the ship that never returned.

And the horses would gently plod on getting slower and slower as the singer continues with each verse and chorus, the song would end, the horses pick up speed, the echoes would die away but the contentment would remain and you would be just another farm lad.